# Student Workbook

to accompany

# Statistics

Sixth Edition

Published by John Wiley & Sons, Inc., Hoboken, New Jersey
Published simultaneously in Canada

For general information on our other products and services, or technical support, please contact our Customer Care Department within the United States at 800-762-2974, outside the United States at 317-572-3993 or fax 317-572-4002.

Wiley also publishes its books in a variety of electronic formats. Some content that appears in print may not be available in electronic books.

For more information about Wiley products, visit our web site at www.wiley.com.

*Library of Congress Cataloging-in-Publication Data:*

10 9 8 7 6 5 4 3 2 1

# Student Workbook
to accompany

# Statistics
**Sixth Edition**

## Robert S. Witte
San Jose State University

## John S. Witte
Case Western Reserve University

Prepared by
## Glenda Streetman Smith, Ph.D.
North Harris College

# PREFACE

This workbook is designed to help you understand and learn the statistical concepts presented in *Statistics*, Sixth Edition.

The first section in each chapter is a set of **Learning Objectives**. This section will give you a clear idea of what you should be able to understand or accomplish when you have studied the chapter.

The second section in the chapter is a set of **Key Terms**. Learning the language of statistics is such an important part of a basic course that the significant vocabulary terms defined in the text are repeated here for further emphasis and exposure. Study these terms carefully.

The third section in each chapter is a **Text Review**. This section does exactly as its name implies; it reviews the most important ideas in the chapter. The blanks that you fill in are there for the purpose of changing the reading/studying experience from a passive process to a more active process. Learning theory tells us that learning is more efficient when the learner is active. Try to fill in each blank as you read, then check your answers at the back of the workbook. Even if you get the answer wrong, the activity will be aiding your learning in the long run.

The fourth section in each chapter consists of **Problems and Exercises**. Some of these are similar to those at the end of the chapter in your text; others will provide somewhat different practice opportunities. Either way, additional practice with these problems and exercises will be a great way to check how much you have learned and to reinforce the learning.

The fifth section is a **Post Test** to check your understanding of the information presented in the chapter. If you do well, you will know that you have mastered some of the most important concepts presented in that chapter. If not, you will know that you need more study time.

The sixth section, **Beyond the Basics,** offers suggestions for advanced students who have mastered the concepts of the chapter and want to explore the ideas further without just working more of the same problems. Those who are really interested in pursuing some of the ideas presented in the text and learning more about the "real world" application of statistics should find this section particularly rewarding. Occasionally this section will contain something just a little different, a hint for how to study particular concepts or a unique presentation of the material.

The answers to the Text Review, Problems and Exercises, and Post Test sections are all in one section at the end of the workbook. The answers to many of the problems were calculated using a computer. If you solve them with a hand calculator, your answers may vary slightly. One way to match more closely is to avoid rounding off at any phase of the problem until the answer is computed. Small differences in rounding during the many steps of some of the more complex calculations can ultimately result in a large discrepancy before the answer is found.

Although every attempt has been made to produce an error-free book, errors do occur, and the author would appreciate hearing from readers about any errors at glenda.smith@nhmccd.edu. Information about all currently detected errors can be obtained by clicking on "Workbook Corrections" in the Web site for this book (http://darwin.cwru.edu/~witte/statistics).

One last word about the problems is necessary. In order to facilitate ease of computation, sample sizes are unrealistically small in many of the problems. Most of the research examples are made up and not necessarily based on real research. If you are interested in some of the ideas presented, do a library search to determine whether any real research has been conducted to investigate the problem of interest. No effort has been made to represent real data from actual studies. The effort has been to provide appropriate practice for students.

# TABLE OF CONTENTS

# CHAPTER 1
# INTRODUCTION

## Learning Objectives

- Develop knowledge and understanding of key terms.
- Given a data set, differentiate between quantitative and qualitative data.
- Given research situations, differentiate between descriptive and inferential statistics.
- Distinguish between independent and dependent variables.

## Key Terms

**Descriptive statistics**—The area of statistics concerned with organizing and summarizing information about a collection of actual observations.

**Inferential statistics**—The area of statistics concerned about generalizing beyond actual observations.

**Data**—A collection of observations from a survey or experiment.

**Quantitative data**—A set of observations where any single observation is a number that represents an amount or a count.

**Qualitative data**—A set of observations where any single observation is a word or code that represents a class or category.

**Variable**—A characteristic or property that can take on different values.

**Constant**—A characteristic or property that can take on only one value.

**Independent variable**—A variable that is manipulated by the investigator.

**Dependent variable**—A variable that is measured, counted, or recorded by the investigator.

**Experiment**—Study with an independent and dependent variable.

**Correlation Study**—Study with two dependent variables.

## Text Review

There are many reasons why you should study statistics. One is that you will become a more informed reader, able to question statistical reports in newspapers and magazines. A second reason is that the study of statistics will help you to read and understand research reports in your particular area of interest. Finally, you may actually one day be involved in planning a statistical analysis for your own research project, especially if you plan to earn an advanced degree.

There are two types of statistics: descriptive and inferential. When a researcher wants to organize or summarize information about a collection of observations, the older area of statistics, (1)_____ statistics would be used. When the researcher must generalize beyond the actual observations, then (2)_____ statistics would be used.

A researcher gathers information in the form of individual records called observations. These records could be IQ scores, height, weight, gas mileage of a particular car, or length of life span of white rats. A collection of observations is referred to as (3)_____. In a set of observations, when any single record is a number that represents an amount or a count, the data are (4)_____. On the other hand, if a single observation is a word or code that represents a class or category, the data are (5)_____.

Numbers may be arbitrarily assigned to survey responses such as *yes* and *no* replies in order to facilitate computer processing. Numbers may also appear in certain instances where they represent only category or classification. An example would be the number on a player's football jersey. The number 88 simply indicates that this player is probably a tight end. It does not indicate that he is twice as good a player as number 44, probably a running back. When numbers are used in this way, they represent (6)_____ data.

An important distinction to the field of research methods is based on two types of variables. The variable that is manipulated by the researcher is called the (7)_____ variable, while the (8) _____ variable is the one measured by the researcher. Investigators conduct experiments using independent and dependent variables in order to establish (9)_____ relationships. Some studies referred to as (10)_____ use two dependent variables and yield less clear-cut conclusions about cause-effect relationships.

## Problems and Exercises

### I. Indicate whether the following data are quantitative or qualitative.
1. Social Security numbers    _____
2. life span of black males    _____
3. weight    _____
4. socioeconomic status    _____
5. eye color    _____
6. years work experience    _____
7. movie ratings (G, PG, PG-13, R, X) _____
8. top ten best sellers    _____
9. scores on a statistics exam    _____
10. average allowance for ten year olds _____

## II. Indicate whether the following situations would require descriptive (D) or inferential (I) statistics.

1.  DI    analysis of the 2000 census
2.  DI    calculation of grade point average
3.  DI    Nielsen ratings for a particular TV show
4.  DI    "best team" award at a swim meet
5.  DI    survey results from a magazine poll
6.  DI    average age of students in your class
7.  DI    dentists' preference for brand of toothpaste
8.  DI    number of football games won by your team
9.  DI    average monthly percent inflation rate
10. DI    finance charge on your charge account

## III. For each of the possible relationships below, indicate whether the corresponding study is an experiment or a correlation study, and if it is an experiment, identify the independent and dependent variables.

1.  relationship between intelligence and reading ability

2.  test anxiety levels among students who undergo hypnosis or not

3.  reaction time and different amounts of alcohol consumed

## Post Test

1. The two main subdivisions of statistics are _____ and _____.

2. _____ is used to organize and summarize data.

3. _____ is used to generalize beyond the actual observations.

4. A collection of observations from a survey or experiment is called _____.

5. A set of observations where any single observation is a number that represents a count or amount is _____ data.

6. A set of observations where any single observation is a word or code that represents a class or category is _____ data.

7. The variable manipulated by the investigator is the _____ variable.

8. A/an _____ (type of study) will allow the investigator to draw cause-effect conclusions.

9. The variable measured by the investigator is called the _____ variable.

10. A study with two dependent variables is a/an _____.

**Beyond the Basics**

In the library, locate some issues of a professional journal that reflect your interest. Look at the methods and results sections of the articles. Determine whether the statistical analysis was descriptive or inferential. Think about the reasons for doing an inferential analysis rather than a descriptive one. Determine whether the data used are quantitative or qualitative. Is the study a correlation or an experiment? Identify the dependent and independent variables.

# CHAPTER 2
# DESCRIBING DATA WITH TABLES

## Learning Objectives

- Develop knowledge and understanding of key terms.

- Given a data set, construct and interpret a frequency distribution for grouped or ungrouped data.

- Interpret frequency distributions constructed by other researchers.

## Key Terms

**Frequency distribution**—A collection of observations produced by sorting observations into classes and showing their frequency (or number) of occurrences in each class.

**Frequency distribution for ungrouped data**—A frequency distribution produced whenever observations are sorted into classes of single values.

**Frequency distribution for grouped data**—A frequency distribution produced whenever observations are sorted into classes of more than one value.

**Unit of measurement**—The smallest possible difference between scores.

**Class interval width**—The distance between the two tabled boundaries, after each boundary has been expanded by one-half of one unit of measurement.

**Outlier**—A very extreme observation.

**Relative frequency distribution**—A frequency distribution showing the frequency of each class as a part or fraction of the total frequency for the entire distribution.

**Cumulative frequency distribution**—A frequency distribution showing the total number of observations in each class and in all lower-ranked classes.

**Percentile rank of an observation**—Percentage of observations in the entire distribution with similar or smaller values than that observation.

## Text Review

There is no single right way to organize data, but a few guidelines make using tables and graphs relatively simple. A frequency distribution for ungrouped data results when observations are sorted into classes of (1)_____ values. Observations are arranged in a column with the (2)_____ observation at the bottom and the (3)_____ at the top. When the number of possible values is larger than twenty, a frequency distribution for (4)_____ data is more appropriate. In this type of distribution, observations are sorted into classes of more than one value.

There are several guidelines for preparing frequency distributions. One is that each observation should be included in only (5)_____ class. The second guideline is that all classes must be listed, even those with zero frequencies. The third guideline states that all classes must be (6)_____ in width. The fourth guideline is optional and suggests that all classes must have both upper and lower (7)_____. The fifth guideline instructs the researcher to select width of classes from (8)_____ numbers. The sixth states that the lower boundary of each class should be a multiple of class width. The seventh guideline indicates that approximately (9)_____ classes is the ideal number. However, this number should be flexible. Larger data sets might require more classes so that important data patterns are not overlooked. Smaller data sets may be more clearly portrayed with fewer classes.

In a well-constructed frequency table, each observation should be clearly assigned to one and only one class and the gaps between classes should always equal one (10)_____ _____ _____.

A (11)_____ frequency distribution shows the frequency of each class as a part or fraction of the total frequency for the entire distribution. This type of distribution helps to compare two distributions based on different numbers of observations. It can also be used to examine the relative concentration of observations among different classes within the same distribution.

A frequency distribution showing the total number of observations at or below each class is a (12)_____ _____ distribution. The most effective use of this type of distribution is with data where relative standing within the distribution is important. A good example would be achievement or aptitude test scores. These cumulative percents are referred to as (13)_____ _____ when they describe the relative position of an observation within the distribution. When obtained from a distribution of ungrouped data, percentile ranks are exact, but when obtained from a distribution of grouped data, they are only (14)_____.

Frequency distributions may be constructed for qualitative data. Note that the numerical summary of qualitative data in this way does not change it to quantitative data. Remember in Chapter 1, the emphasis was on a single observation when determining whether a set of observations represented qualitative or quantitative data. When qualitative data can be ranked, the data should be listed in (15)_____ order in the frequency table. The ranking of qualitative data makes it possible to construct cumulative frequency distributions, but (16)_____ _____ distributions can be constructed for qualitative data even when it cannot be ranked.

Occasionally an extreme observation will appear in a data set. Such extreme observations, called (17)_____, should always be checked for accuracy.

When viewing a frequency distribution for the first time, it is important to look at the entire table. The reader should examine the title, column headings, and (18)_____. Then note the overall appearance, including whether or not the distribution is balanced around one or more peaks. Keep an open mind and formulate questions as you examine a distribution.

**Guidelines for Frequency Distributions**
1. Each observation should be included in one, and only one, class.
2. List all classes, even those with zero frequencies.
3. All classes (with upper and lower boundaries) should be equal in width.
4. All classes should have both an upper and a lower boundary.
5. Select the width of classes from convenient numbers.
6. The lower boundary of each class should be a multiple of the class width.
7. In general, aim for a total of approximately ten classes.

## How to Construct a Frequency Distribution

1. Find the range, that is, the difference between the largest and smallest observation.
2. Find the class width required to span the data range by dividing the range by the desired number of classes.
3. Round off to the nearest convenient width.
4. Determine where the lowest class should begin.
5. Determine where the lowest class should end by adding the class width to the lower boundary and then subtracting one unit of measurement.
6. Working upward, list as many equivalent classes as are required to include the largest observation.
7. Indicate with a tally the class in which each observation falls.
8. Replace the tally count for each class with a frequency.
9. Supply headings for both columns and a title for the table.

## Problems and Exercises

1. On a fifty-point exam for a general psychology class, a professor observes the following results. Construct a frequency distribution. Also construct a relative frequency distribution, a cumulative frequency distribution, and a cumulative relative frequency distribution.

| 48 | 37 | 22 | 38 | 39 | 45 | 42 | 29 | 48 | 33 |
| 41 | 40 | 34 | 30 | 39 | 38 | 42 | 44 | 32 | 31 |
| 35 | 40 | 36 | 42 | 30 | 33 | 41 | 46 | 29 | 39 |

## Table 2.1

| A | B | C | D | E |
|---|---|---|---|---|
| grades | f | relative f | cumulative f | cumulative % |

2. Which class interval would contain the score closest to the 50th percentile?

3. Which is appropriate for this data set, a grouped or ungrouped distribution? Why?

4. Describe any interesting patterns. In general, will the professor be pleased with this overall class performance?

5. What is the unit of measure for this data set?

6. A third grader's reading achievement test score is reported to his mother as a score at the 73rd percentile. What is the meaning of this score? If his math score is at the 66th percentile, relatively speaking, is he better in math or reading?

## Post Test

1. When observations are sorted into classes of single values, the result is referred to as a _____.

2. A frequency distribution for grouped data should be used when there are more than _____ possible values.

3. A problem sometimes encountered when data are grouped is

_____.

4. When too many classes are used, a problem sometimes encountered is

_____.

5. The size of the gap between classes should always equal

_____.

6. _____ distributions can be especially useful when comparing the shapes of two or more distributions with unequal numbers of observations.

7. _____ _____ indicates the percentage of observations in the distribution with similar or smaller values.

8. Cumulative frequency distributions can only be constructed for qualitative data if the data can be _____.

9. A very extreme observation is called a/an _____.

---

**Beyond the Basics**
Obtain your own data set by asking thirty people to count the change in their purse or pocket for you. Record their responses and construct a frequency distribution. Note any patterns. Were there any outliers present? If so, can you explain?

# CHAPTER 3
# DESCRIBING DATA WITH GRAPHS

## Learning Objectives

- Develop knowledge and understanding of key terms.

- Construct and interpret histograms, bar graphs, frequency polygons, and stem and leaf displays.

- Recognize skewness in a distribution and determine the direction.

- Recognize misleading graphs.

## Key Terms

**Histogram**—Bar-type graph for quantitative data. No gaps between adjacent bars.

**Frequency polygon**—Line graph for quantitative data.

**Stem and leaf display**—A device for sorting quantitative data on the basis of leading and trailing digits.

**Positively skewed distribution**—A distribution that includes a few extreme observations with relatively large values in the positive direction.

**Negatively skewed distribution**—A distribution that includes a few extreme observations with relatively small values in the negative direction.

**Bar graph**—Bar-type graph for qualitative data. Gaps between adjacent bars.

## Text Review

Making graphs from (1)_____ _____
helps to describe data more clearly. A bar-type graph appropriate for
quantitative data is called a (2)_____. This graph is
characterized by (3)_____ units along the horizontal axis that
indicate (4)_____ _____. The equal units
along the vertical axis indicate (5)_____ _____ _____.

Where the two axes meet, both frequency and class interval equal (6)_____.
Along the horizontal axis, values always (7)_____ from
left to right.

The line graph, or (8)_____ _____, is a
variation of the histogram that is particularly useful when comparing
(9)_____.

Finally, quantitative data can be summarized using a (10)_____
_____ _____ _____, which is somewhat of a cross
between a (11)_____ _____ and a (12)_____.
The advantage of the stem and leaf display is in summarizing data without
losing information from the (13)_____ _____.

(14)_____ is an important characteristic of a frequency distribution,
no matter how it is presented. The normal shape, which looks like a
(15)_____, reflects the actual distribution of many familiar data
sets. Standardized test scores are usually represented by the normal curve.

The (16)_____ shape, with two humps, reflects the presence of two different types of observations in the same distribution. A lopsided shape with many observations to the left indicates the presence of many smaller values and only a few large values. This is referred to as (17)_____ skewed. A lopsided shape with many observations to the right indicates the presence of many larger values and only a few small values. This is referred to as (18)_____ skewed. Thus, skewness, unlike most other concepts, is defined by the (19)_____ of observations, not the majority.

Qualitative data can be depicted more clearly using a (20)_____ _____. The horizontal axis reflects (21)_____ _____ and the vertical axis (22)_____, just as in a histogram. Unlike the histogram, however, the bar graph has (23)_____ between the bars, indicating the discontinuous nature of qualitative data.

Misleading graphs can be constructed to support a particular point of view. The correct method of constructing a graph is to make the horizontal and vertical axes (24)_____ _____ in height and width. The bars on the graph must also be (25)_____ _____ in width. And the entire scale must be reproduced beginning with (26)_____, unless there is a break in scale clearly indicated.

## Problems and Exercises

### Constructing Graphs
1. Decide on the appropriate type of graph.
2. Use a ruler to draw the horizontal and vertical axes (equal width and height).
3. Identify the string of class intervals that eventually will be superimposed on the horizontal axis.
4. Superimpose the string of class intervals (with gaps for bar graphs) along the entire length of the horizontal axis.
5. Along the entire length of the vertical axis, superimpose a progression of convenient numbers beginning with zero.
6. Using the scaled axes, construct bars to reflect the frequency of observations within each class interval.
7. Supply labels for both axes and a title for the graph.

1. A market research firm is hired to compare consumer preferences as to comfort and ease of driving of four different vehicles. The following results are obtained. Construct a bar graph describing these results.

| Vehicle | Number of Housewives Preferring |
|---|---|
| Four-wheel drive | 36 |
| Van | 44 |
| Sports car | 24 |
| Pick-up truck | 13 |

2. The Keebler elves are being evaluated on a ten-point scale for cookie-packing aptitude. The following ratings are observed:

| 10 | 4 | 3 | 6 | 5 | 6 | 1 | 6 | 7 | 7 |
|----|---|---|---|---|---|---|---|---|---|
| 6  | 9 | 2 | 8 | 5 | 3 | 6 | 9 | 8 | 4 |
| 9  | 5 | 1 | 5 | 2 | 1 | 3 | 8 | 3 | 7 |

a. Construct a histogram for the above data.
b. Construct a frequency polygon.

3. In a statistics class at a community college, approximately half the students are nontraditional (about age 30 or older) and the other half, traditional (age 19 or 20). The students earn the following scores on the first exam:

**Nontraditional Students**

69 68 77 94 76
88 76 75 79 69
79 66 98 72 83
81 81 82 83 92
86 92 77 82 71

**Traditional Students**

67 87 98 78 77
83 84 87 77 90
78 76 78 70 72
74 75 66 70 70
68 66 84 66 67

a. Using the preceding data, construct frequency polygons on the same graph showing the test results achieved by the two groups.
b. What is the shape of the distribution for nontraditional students?
c. What is the shape of the distribution for traditional students?
d. Overall, is the performance of the two groups similar or dissimilar?

## Post Test

1. What determines whether to construct a bar graph or histogram for a given data set?

2. List three ways to construct graphs so that they are misleading.

3. What determines whether skewness of a distribution is positive or negative?

4. When is it beneficial to construct a frequency polygon instead of a histogram?

5. Why does a bar graph have gaps between the bars when a histogram does not?

6. What is the biggest advantage of a stem and leaf display?

**Beyond the Basics**
Look for histograms, bar graphs, or frequency polygons in current newspapers or magazines. Are there any features intended to be misleading? How might the use of computers have affected the presentation of misleading graphs?

# CHAPTER 4
# DESCRIBING DATA WITH AVERAGES

## Learning Objectives

- Develop knowledge and understanding of key terms.
- Calculate and interpret the various measures of central tendency.
- Determine appropriate measures of central tendency for specific data sets.

## Key Terms

**Measures of central tendency**—General term for the various averages.

**Mode**—The value of the most frequent observation.

**Bimodal**—Describes any distribution with two obvious peaks.

**Median**—The middle value when observations are ordered from least to most, or vice versa.

**Population**—A complete set of observations.

**Sample**—A subset of observations from a population.

**Sample mean**—The balance point for a sample, found by dividing the total value of all observations in the sample by the sample size.

**Sample size**—The total number of observations in the sample.

**Population mean**—The balance point for a population, found by dividing the total value of all observations in the population by the population size.

**Population size**—The total number of observations in the population.

## Text Review

There are several types of averages, all known as (1)_____
_____ _____ _____. The most frequently
occurring observation is an average called the (2)_____. It is
understood as the most (3)_____. Sometimes a distribution will
have more than one mode. If there are two peaks, distributions are referred to
as (4)_____. If there are more than two peaks, the distribution is
referred to as (5)_____. The occurrence of more than one
mode may indicate (6)_____ in the data set.

When observations are ordered from least to most, the middle value is the
(7)_____. The median has a percentile rank of (8)_____. The
median reflects the (9)_____ of an observation, not the position.

The most common of the averages is the (10)_____. Adding all the
observations and then dividing by the number of observations will yield the
(11)_____. This calculation can be done without ordering the data or
organizing it. The symbol for the sample mean is (12)_____. Another
important symbol is the one for "the sum of," (13)_____. The symbol
(14)_____ represents any unspecified observation. The mean serves as
the balance point for a distribution. This is true because the sum of all
observations, expressed as positive and negative deviations from the mean,
always equals (15)_____. Statisticians actually deal with two types
of means. One is the mean of a complete set of observations or a
(16) _____. The other is a (17)_____ mean,
or the mean of a subset of observations from a population. These two means
are distinguished by different symbols but are calculated by the same formula.

Similar values of the mode, median, and mean will usually indicate that the distribution is (18)_____ _____ _____. In this case, any of the measures of central (19)_____ can be used to describe the distribution. If a distribution is skewed by extreme observations, the values of the three measures of (20)_____

_____ differ considerably. Since the (21)_____ and the (22)_____ are not sensitive to extreme observations, the (23)_____ should be reported along with the median. Accordingly, large differences between the mean and the median signal a (24)_____ distribution. If the mean is larger than the median, the distribution will be (25)_____ skewed, but if the median is larger than the mean, the distribution will be (26)_____ skewed. Overall, the (27)_____ is the most preferred average.

For qualitative data, the (28)_____ is always appropriate. However, the (29)_____ is only appropriate if the data can be ordered. Conventional usage prescribes that the term "average" usually refers to the (30)_____.

## Problems and Exercises

1. A number of college students were surveyed to determine what type of music they most often purchase. For the following results, which type of average is appropriate and why?

    a. Rap          135
    b. Blues         98
    c. Classical     53
    d. Rock         222

5. The sleep research center at a medical school selected volunteers for research. The ages of the volunteers follow below. Compute the mean, median, and mode.

22, 45, 34, 25, 23, 36, 23, 38, 27, 32, 44, 55

3. Students were asked to report the number of hours per week spent studying for psychology. Calculate the mean, median, and mode.

6, 4, 9, 5, 6, 6, 2, 6, 4, 5, 8, 8, 7, 9, 3

4. Students earned the following grades on the first statistics exam of the term. Calculate the mean, median, and mode.

98, 85, 93, 77, 76, 99, 89, 75, 93, 92, 90, 77, 93, 86

5. Ten preschool children on a playground were asked to guess their mother's age. Calculate the mean, median, and mode of their guesses.

37, 20, 33, 50, 100, 10, 40, 18, 25, 20

## Post Test

1. What measure(s) of central tendency are best when extreme observations are present in the data set?



2. What measure of central tendency is appropriate for qualitative data?



3. _____ is the most frequently occurring observation.


4. What is the symbol for the sample mean? _____


5. What is the formula for the mean? _____


6. What does a bimodal distribution suggest about the data set?


7. What measure(s) of central tendency should be reported for a skewed distribution?


8. The single most preferred average is the _____.


9. When the median exceeds the mean, the distribution is _____ skewed.

## Beyond the Basics

Chapter 4 introduces both the first symbols and the first formula. Here is a hint about memorizing them. Get some 3 x 5 cards. On one side of a card write the symbol or formula. On the other side, write the meaning of the symbol or some pertinent information about the formula. Study them just as you did flash cards when you were younger. The type of rote learning required for this information is often tedious. You will learn best from frequent repetitions of short duration. The 3 x 5 cards are easy to put in your purse or pocket. Keep them handy for frequent review whenever you have a few spare minutes. This type of review will be far more effective than hours of concentrated time. You may recall from a General Psychology class the proven learning principle that distributed practice is more effective than massed practice. Here is an opportunity to put that principle to practical use.

# CHAPTER 5
# DESCRIBING VARIABILITY

## Learning Objectives

- Develop knowledge and understanding of the key terms.

- Calculate and interpret the various measures of variability.

## Key Terms

**Measures of variability**—General term for various measures of the amount of variation or differences among observations in a distribution.

**Range**—The difference between the largest and smallest observations.

**Variance**—The mean of all squared deviations from the mean.

**Standard deviation**—A rough measure of the average amount by which observations deviate on either side of their mean.

**Sample standard deviation**—A rough measure of the average amount by which observations in the sample deviate on either side of the sample mean.

**Population standard deviation**—A rough measure of the average amount by which observations in the population deviate on either side of the population mean.

**Interquartile range (IQR)**—The range for the middle 50 percent of all observations.

## Text Review

An exact measure of variability representing the difference between the largest and smallest observation is the (1)_____. The range has the advantage of being easily understood and easily (2)_____.

However, it also has shortcomings. One weakness is that it is based on (3)_____ _____ _____. In addition, the value of the range tends to (4)_____ as the number of observations increases.

The (5)_____ _____ is the preferred measure of (6)_____ and holds the same exalted position as the (7)_____ holds among measures of central tendency. There are two formulas for calculating the standard deviation, the (8)_____ formula, which helps to understand the origin of the standard deviation, and the (9)_____ formula, which is better to use for calculation when the mean is a complex number or the number of observations is large. The standard deviation is simply the (10)_____ _____ of the (11)_____. The standard deviation has the advantage of expressing the observations in (12)_____ units of measure. The standard deviation may be thought of as a (13)_____ measure of the (14)_____ amount by which observations deviate from their (15)_____.

For most frequency distributions, a majority of observations, as many as (16)_____ percent, are within one standard deviation of the mean. By the same token, a minority, as few as (17)_____ percent, will deviate more than two standard deviations from the mean.

31

The mean is a measure of (18)_____, and the standard deviation is a measure of (19)_____ from the mean. Standard deviations may be expressed as positive or (20)_____ deviations from the mean. However, standard deviations cannot be negative numbers. The positive and negative signs indicate direction from the mean.

An important spin-off of the range is the (21)_____ _____, which represents the range for the middle (22)_____ _____ of the distribution. Like the range, the interquartile range is fairly easy to calculate, but unlike the range, it is not sensitive to (23)_____ _____. Therefore, the interquartile range might be especially appropriate when there are (24)_____ in the distribution.

Measures of variability for qualitative data are virtually (25)_____. However, descriptive terms, such as maximum, minimum, or intermediate variability, can be used to describe variability for qualitative data.

## Problems and Exercises

1. The following data represent the weights of twelve three-year-olds placed in foster homes by a social worker. Compute the mean and standard deviation.

   22, 45, 34, 25, 23, 36, 23, 38, 27, 32, 44, 55,

2. Round off the mean and the standard deviation in problem 1 to the nearest whole numbers (mean = 34 and standard deviation = 10) and answer the following questions.

    a. Between what two scores would 68 percent of the observations fall?

    b. Beyond what scores would 5 percent or less of the scores fall?

    c. What score would be one standard deviation above the mean?

    d. Where would a score of 40 fall?

    e. Where would a score of 21 fall?

3. Compute the range for the following data:

22, 45, 34, 25, 23, 36, 23, 38, 27, 32, 44, 55

4. Compute the range and standard deviation for the following data:

| 21 | 38 | 14 | 22 | 33 | 17 | 19 | 26 | 31 |
|----|----|----|----|----|----|----|----|----|
| 28 | 25 | 19 | 12 | 12 | 24 | 36 | 20 | 32 |

5. Compute the range and standard deviation for the following set of exam scores:

82, 91, 64, 77, 84, 93, 58, 76, 73, 89, 81, 67

## Post Test

1. What are two limitations of the range?

2. Which is the preferred measure of variability for quantitative data? Why?

3. What measures of variability are appropriate for qualitative data?

4. What conditions indicate that the computation formula should be used to calculate standard deviation?

5. What is the advantage of the interquartile range?

---

**Beyond the Basics**

Two statistics classes have taken their first exam, and both classes scored a mean of 78. In class A, the standard deviation was 5 points, and in class B the standard deviation was 8 points. If your grade were 74, which class would you rather be in? If your grade were 87, which class would you rather be in? Does the standard deviation make a difference in your answer even though the two class means were the same? Why?

---

# CHAPTER 6

# NORMAL DISTRIBUTIONS (I): BASICS

## Learning Objectives

- Develop knowledge and understanding of key terms.

- Understand the theoretical concepts of the normal curve and the standard normal table.

- Calculate and interpret $z$ scores.

## Key Terms

**Normal curve**—A theoretical curve noted for its symmetrical bell-shaped form.

**z score**—A score that indicates how many standard deviations an observation is above or below the mean of the distribution.

**Standard normal curve**—The one tabled normal curve with a mean of 0 and a standard deviation of 1.

## Text Review

The normal curve is a (1)_____ curve noted for its (2) _____ bell-shaped form. Because of the symmetrical shape, the lower half is a (3)_____ image of the upper half. The curve peaks at a point (4)_____ along the horizontal spread and then tapers off at each end. Theoretically, these tails of the curve extend (5)_____, as they never touch the horizontal axis. In order to use the normal curve, we must assume that a set of quantitative data is (6)_____

_____. We must also have the values of the (7)
_____ and the (8)_____ _____.

Another requirement for using the normal curve is that the original observations must be expressed as (9)_____ _____, indicating how many standard deviations an observation is from the (10) _____. The $z$ score always indicates the value of the original score relative to its (11)_____ and (12)_____

_____.

The standard normal curve always has a mean of (13)_____ and a standard deviation of (14)_____. A major advantage of using the standard normal curve is that a table is available from which we can determine the proportion represented by area under the curve at any position on the horizontal axis marked by a particular $z$ score. The standard normal table consists of columns of $z$ scores coordinated with columns of (15)_____.

In the standard normal table, columns B and B' represent the proportion of area under the normal curve between the mean and a $z$ score value. Columns C and C' represent the area between the $z$ score and the tail of the curve. Always remember that the B and C columns in each half will sum to (16)_____, and the total area under the normal curve always equals (17)_____.

## Problems and Exercises

1. Assume that ACT (American College Test) composite scores approximate a normal curve with a mean of 18 and a standard deviation of 6. Convert the following ACT scores to $z$ scores.
   a.  32
   b.  21
   c.  14
   d.  25
   e.  16

2. Practice using the standard normal table by answering the following questions.

   a.  What proportion of observations in a normal distribution would you find above a $z$ score of 1.33?

   b.  What proportion of observations in a normal distribution would you find below a $z$ score of .77?

   c.  What proportion of observations in a normal distribution would you find between the mean and a $z$ score of +.50?

   d.  What proportion of observations in a normal distribution would you find between the mean and a $z$ score of -3.10?

## Post Test

1.  The normal curve is a theoretical curve noted for being

    _____.

2.  In order to solve problems using the normal curve, one must have the

    values of the _____ and the _____

    _____.

3.  A _____ _____ indicates how many standard deviation units an
    observation is from its mean.

4.  The one tabled normal curve with a mean of 0 and a standard deviation of

    1 is the _____ _____ _____.

5.  In the standard normal table, _____ _____ would be used to
    determine the proportion of area under the curve between the mean and a
    particular z score.

6.  The total area under the curve from the mean to the tail on the left (the
    lower half) represents _____ proportion of the whole curve.

7.  The total area under the curve always equals _____.

---

**Beyond the Basics**

Ask professors from three of your classes to help you with this problem. You
will need to know the mean and standard deviation on the last exam you took
in each course, as well as your own score. If the professor has not calculated
this information, perhaps the data can be made available without disclosing
the identity of other students so that you can calculate the mean and standard
deviation yourself. Using this information, compute your own z score for each
course. Determine which class represents your best performance.

# CHAPTER 7
# NORMAL DISTRIBUTIONS (II): APPLICATIONS

## Learning Objectives

- Develop knowledge and understanding of key terms.
- Solve a variety of problems using the standard normal table.

## Key Terms

Review Key Terms from Chapters 4, 5, and 6. You will need to be well acquainted with all of them to do well in Chapter 7.

## Text Review

Using the standard normal table, it is possible to solve two types of problems. The first type of problem is finding (1) _____, or area under the curve, and the second type is finding (2) _____. It is important to look for the (3) _____ in solving these problems, and not just to memorize. Another helpful technique is to draw or sketch the (4)_____ _____ and shade a target area. This helps to visualize the solution to the problem.

There are four steps to solving problems that require finding proportions. Step one is to (5) _____ the normal curve. Step two is planning a (6)_____ according to the normal table. In step three, the original observations or values of $X$ must be converted to (7) _____ _____. Finally, in step four, you are ready to find the target area. There is usually more than one correct way to solve a normal curve problem.

Remember that the numerical scale along the baseline of the normal curve always increases from left to right. Therefore, the area to the left of a score will represent the proportion of (8) _____ scores and the area to the right will represent the proportion of larger scores.

In addition to finding proportions above and below $z$ scores, it is possible to find proportions of scores between and beyond $z$ scores as well. Usually key words within a problem will help you determine exactly what proportion you are looking for.

The second type of problem we can solve using the normal table is finding (9) _____. Solving this type of problem requires that we enter the table at columns B, B', C, or C' and read the $z$ scores listed in column A. Remember that the (10) _____ of a normal curve always splits the total area into two equal halves, with proportions .5000 to the left of the mean and .5000 to the right of the mean. Also, remember that (11)_____ $z$ scores are associated with the upper or right half and (12) _____ $z$ scores are associated with the lower or left half.

There are four steps to solving these problems. Step one is to sketch the normal curve. Step two is planning a solution. Step three is finding the $z$ score, not by calculation, but by reading it from the normal table. Step four is calculating the score.

In statistics, the middle 95 percent of a distribution is identified with (13)_____ events, while the extreme 2.5 percent in each tail is identified with (14) _____ events.

# Problems and Exercises

1. Finding the proportion for a score left of the mean. Assume that women's shoe sizes approximate a normal distribution with a mean of 7 and a standard deviation of 1.5. What proportion of women will wear size 5 or smaller?

   **Step 1**—Sketch the normal curve and identify the target area.

   **Step 2**—Express the size 5 (target score) as a $z$ score.

   **Step 3**—In column A of the standard normal table, locate the $z$ score of 1.33. From the sketch in step 1, you should see that you are looking for an area at the tail of the curve to the left of the mean. Therefore, you would read the proportion value in C' corresponding to the $z$ score of -1.33. The answer is .0918, or 9%.

   Now try one on your own. Using the same data as in problem 1, what proportion of women will wear size 4.5 or smaller? Follow the same steps as above. Sketching the normal curve is extremely important, as it helps you with a visual interpretation. Don't be tempted to omit this step.

2. Finding the proportion for a score right of the mean. Using the data from problem 1, what proportion of women wear shoes size 9 or smaller?

**Step 1**—Sketch the normal curve as presented earlier.

**Step 2**—Express the size 9 as a $z$ score.

**Step 3**—In column A of the standard normal table, locate the $z$ score of 1.33. From your sketch in step 1, you should see that you are looking for the area that includes all the lower half of the curve plus the area from the mean to the position of the $z$ score. Therefore, you must take the value from column B that corresponds to the $z$ score of 1.33 (.4082) and add it to .5000 (the proportion value of the lower half of the curve). The answer is .9082 or, rounding off, 91 percent of women wear shoes size 9 or smaller. It is little wonder that women with larger feet have trouble finding shoes, because they represent only 9% of the market.
Now try one on your own.

What proportion of women wear size 8 or smaller?

3. Finding scores. Assume that American College Test (ACT) scores approximate a normal curve with a mean of 18 and a standard deviation of 6. Because of overcrowding, a small college wants to use the test to select applicants who score in the top 25%. What would be the appropriate cutoff score?

**Step 1**—Sketch the normal curve and identify the target area.

**Step 2**—Find $z$ in the standard normal table. Since you are looking for the top 25%, you would be looking for .25 in column C. Locate this figure and the corresponding $z$ score. Note that .25 is not listed exactly. Instead, you must choose between .2514 and .2483. You should use .2514, as it is closer in value to .2500. The corresponding $z$ score is .67.

**Step 3**—Convert $z$ to the target score ($X$).

$$\bar{X} = 18 + (.67)(6) = 18 + 4.02 = 22.02$$

Rounding off, this gives us the answer. The college should set its cutoff score at 22. Now try one on your own. Suppose the same college wants to select students for an honors program. If they want students whose scores are in the top 7%, what cutoff score would they use? (Hint: Remember that 7% is .07 proportion.)

The "Soon 2 B Slim" diet program suggests that its followers lose a mean of 15 pounds in the first six weeks of dieting, with a standard deviation of 2 pounds. Use this information to answer questions 4, 5, and 6.

4. Bill lost 19 pounds in his first six weeks. What proportion of dieters lost more than he did?

5. Sandra lost 12 pounds in the first six weeks of dieting. What proportion of dieters would lose between the mean of 15 pounds and her loss of 12 pounds?

6. Fred was the star of the "Soon 2 B Slim" diet and lost more weight than 87 percent of the patrons. How much weight did he lose?

## Post Test

1. What is the purpose of sketching the normal curve as a step in problem solving?

2. What two types of problems can be solved using the normal curve?

3. When reading from left to right, does the numerical scale along the base of the normal curve increase or decrease?

4. Positive $z$ score values correspond to area _____ the mean and negative $z$ scores correspond to area below the mean of the normal curve.

**Beyond the Basics**

In this section in Chapter 6, you were asked to get the necessary data from three of your classes so that you could compute your own $z$ score for each course and determine which class represents your best performance relative to your classmates. Take this exercise one step further by assuming scores are normally distributed, and calculate the proportion of your classmates that scored above and below your score in each class.

# CHAPTER 8
# MORE ABOUT $z$ SCORES

## Learning Objectives

- Develop knowledge and understanding of key terms.

- Understand the use of $z$ scores for non-normal distributions.

- Understand the use of standard scores and know how to make standard score conversions.

## Key Terms

**Standard score**—Any score expressed relative to a known mean and a known standard deviation.

**Transformed standard score**—A standard score that, unlike a $z$ score, usually lacks negative signs and decimal points.

**Percentile ranks**—The percentile rank of a score indicates the percentage of scores in the entire distribution with similar or smaller values.

## Text Review

It is possible to use $z$ scores with non-normal distributions, but when doing so, the (1)_____ _____ _____ cannot be consulted. This is true because the shape of the $z$ score distribution will be the same as the original distribution. However, no matter what the shape of the distribution, the conversion to $z$ scores always produces a distribution with a mean of (2)_____ and a standard deviation of (3)_____.

Using $z$ scores is helpful in interpreting test scores, especially when examining a person's strengths and weaknesses on several different tests. However, using $z$ scores requires that a (4)_____ group be specified providing a standard for comparison of various test performances.

Whenever scores are expressed relative to a known mean and standard deviation, they are called (5)_____ scores. A $z$ score qualifies as a standard score because it has a known mean of zero and a standard deviation of one. A $z$ score can be converted to other types of standard scores that do not have (6)_____ or (7) _____ _____. This type of transformation does not change the shape of the distribution or the relative standing of the individual scores within the distribution. $T$ scores are a standard score transformation that has a mean of (8)_____ and a standard deviation of (9)_____. Other familiar pairs of numbers representing respective means and standard deviations have been established for (10)_____ scores and (11)_____ scores.

Original scores may also be interpreted as percentile ranks. The percentile rank of a score indicates the percentage of scores in the entire distribution with similar or smaller values. The median score of a distribution will always have a percentile rank of (12)_____. Percentile ranks do have limitations. The scale of percentile ranks does not increase in value in an orderly way as do the scales for (13)_____ _____. For this reason, many people who regularly deal with test scores prefer the use of standard scores.

## Problems and Exercises

1. In Chapter 6, you were given the following problem. Assume that ACT composite scores approximate a normal curve with a mean of 18 and a standard deviation of 6. Convert the following ACT scores to $z$ scores. The correct $z$ scores are now given with the ACT scores. This time, convert the $z$ scores to $T$ scores. Hint: this is done using formula 8.1, substituting the $T$ score mean of 50 and the standard deviation of 10 in the appropriate places.

   a. 32          $z = 2.33$
   b. 21          $z = .50$
   c. 14          $z = -.67$
   d. 25          $z = 1.17$
   e. 16          $z = -.33$

2. Find the percentile rank for the following GRE scores. Remember that GRE scores are standard scores with a mean of 500 and a standard deviation of 100. You will need to convert the scores to $z$ scores and then use the standard normal table. Remember that any score above the mean must have .5000 added to the proportion from the table, because the table represents only one-half of the entire distribution.

   a. 550
   b. 620
   c. 370

3. What IQ scores would represent the following percentile ranks? Remember that these are just normal curve problems. You must use the mean of 100 and standard deviation of 15 appropriate for IQ scores.

    a. 84
    b. 50
    c. 35

4. A biochemical research lab wishes to hire a young scientist and asks your help in determining which applicant is the brightest. (Assume that brightness corresponds to performance on standardized tests.) Which of the following applicants do you recommend? Hint: You must convert all three scores to $z$ scores.

Jim—GRE score of 640

Bob—ACT score of 27

Mary—IQ of 125

## Post Test

1. Discuss the use of $z$ scores with non-normal distributions.

2. No matter what the shape of the original distribution, a conversion to $z$ scores always creates a distribution with a mean of _____ and a standard deviation of _____.

3. What information is required for the use of $z$ scores in interpreting test scores?

4. What is the advantage of $T$ scores?

5. What is the most serious limitation of percentile ranks when comparing scores based on normal distributions?

---

**Beyond the Basics**

Chapter 8 includes a discussion of number pairs that are frequently substituted to create standard score transformations. Those listed are for IQ scores, GRE scores, and $T$ scores. By checking in the library in such sources as the Boroughs Mental Measurement Yearbook, or by talking with a person involved in testing such as a high school counselor, director of the college testing center, or a psychologist, try to determine other values that can be substituted to create different commonly used standard scores.

# CHAPTER 9

# DESCRIBING RELATIONSHIPS: CORRELATION

## Learning Objectives

- Develop knowledge and understanding of key terms.

- Calculate and interpret Pearson correlation coefficients.

- Interpret scatterplots.

- Become familiar with other types of correlations.

## Key Terms

**Positive relationship**—Occurs in so far as pairs of observations tend to occupy similar relative positions in their respective distributions.

**Negative relationship**—Occurs in so far as pairs of observations tend to occupy dissimilar and opposite positions in their respective distributions.

**Scatterplot**—A graph containing a cluster of dots that represents all pairs of observations.

**Pearson correlation coefficient**—A number between -1 and +1 that describes the linear relationship between pairs of quantitative variables.

**Linear relationship**—A relationship that can be described with a straight line.

**Curvilinear relationship**—A relationship that can be described with a curved line.

**Correlation coefficient (r)**—A number between -1 and +1 that describes the relationship between pairs of variables.

**Correlation matrix**—Table showing correlations for all possible pairs of variables.

## Text Review

In previous chapters, we have examined individual data sets representing collections of records or observations of some characteristic that varied among individuals (e.g., height, weight, and IQ scores, or popping time for kernels of corn and average burning time for light bulbs). In statistics, since the values of these characteristics vary among individuals, they are commonly referred to as variables. In Chapter 9 we will examine relationships between two variables. Therefore, we will see pairs of observations.

When relatively high values of one variable are paired with relatively high values of the other variable, and low values are paired with low values, the relationship is (1)_____.

Another way to think of this is that values of one variable increase as values of the other increase, while values of one variable decrease as values of the other decrease. An example of a positive relationship between two variables would be study time and performance in statistics class. As study time increases, performance in class will also increase. Thus, relatively high values of each variable are paired and relatively low values of each are paired.

When pairs of observations occupy dissimilar and opposite relative positions in their respective distributions, the relationship is (2)_____. An example of a negative relationship would be auto gas mileage and horsepower. As horsepower is increased, gas mileage would be expected to decrease. Conversely, when horsepower is decreased, gas mileage should increase.

It may occur to you that certain variables may exist which would not be related either positively or negatively. This happens to be true. Consider, for example, hat size and IQ. Pairs of these variables would not occupy either similar or dissimilar positions in their respective distributions. If the pairs were graphed on a scatterplot, no pattern would appear. These variables would be said to have no relationship. A calculated correlation coefficient for the two variables would be near zero.

The graph that shows the relationship between variables as a cluster of dots is called a (3)_____. The pattern formed by the dot cluster is significant. If the cluster has a slope from upper right to lower left, it depicts a (4)_____ relationship. If the slope is from upper left to lower right, the relationship is (5)_____. A dot cluster that lacks any apparent slope reflects (6)_____ _____. The more closely a dot cluster approximates a straight line, the (7)_____ the relationship. When a relationship can be described with a straight line, it is described as (8)_____. When the dot cluster forms a curved line, the relationship is said to be (9)_____.

The relationship between two variables that represent quantitative data is described by a correlation coefficient and designated by the symbol (10)_____. The correlation coefficient ranges in value from (11)_____ to (12)_____. The sign of $r$ indicates whether the relationship is (13)_____ or (14)_____. The value of $r$ indicates the (15)_____ of the relationship. The correlation coefficient is referred to as the (16)_____ _____ and was named after the British scientist Karl Pearson.

Interpretation of $r$ is related to the direction and strength of the correlation. The direction, either (17)_____ or (18)_____, is indicated by the sign of the correlation coefficient. The strength is reflected by the (19)_____ of $r$. An $r$ value of .50 or more in either direction is typical of important relationships in most areas of behavioral and educational research. The value of $r$ cannot be interpreted as a proportion or percent of some perfect relationship.

The Pearson $r$ can be calculated using a $z$ score formula, but this is never actually done in practice, partly because of the extra effort required to convert the original data into $z$ scores. The value of the $z$ score formula lies more in aiding with the understanding of correlation. The correlation coefficient is actually calculated using the computation formula.

One important concept to keep in mind is that a correlation coefficient never provides information about cause and effect. Cause and effect can only be proved by (20)_____ _____.

There are other types of correlation coefficients designed for use in various situations. For example, when the data consists of ranks, a (21)_____ _____ correlation is used. When one variable is quantitative and the other is qualitative, the result is a (22) _____ _____ correlation coefficient. If both variables represent ordered qualitative data, the resulting correlation coefficient is called (23) _____ _____.

When every possible pairing of variables is reported, a (24)_____ _____ is produced. A correlation matrix is particularly useful when many variables are being studied.

# Problems and Exercises

**Some hints for computing and interpreting correlation coefficients:**

a. Since a correlation coefficient always has a value between -1 and +1, you will know you have made an error if your answer is outside this range.
b. It may help to sketch a scatter plot before you start computing. This would help you to estimate whether the *r* value will be positive or negative and how strong the relationship may be.
c. When computing *r*, remember that *n* represents number of pairs of *X* and *Y* values.

1. A physical education teacher believes that eye-hand coordination is an important factor in performance in both shooting a basketball and pitching horseshoes. Eight student volunteers achieved the following results out of fifteen tries each at shooting the basketball and pitching horseshoes.
   a. Compute a Pearson *r*.
   b. In reality, eye-hand coordination probably is related to performance in both sports. What possible explanation can you offer for the negative correlation obtained in this particular instance?

   **Basketball     Horseshoes**

   | $X$ | $Y$ |
   |-----|-----|
   | 8   | 2   |
   | 10  | 3   |
   | 7   | 3   |
   | 6   | 5   |
   | 7   | 6   |
   | 4   | 8   |
   | 2   | 9   |
   | 3   | 10  |

2. Sketch a scatterplot that depicts the relationship for problem 1.

3. A statistics professor asked her students to record the number of hours spent studying for an exam. She then computed $r$ for the correlation between hours spent studying and exam grades.
   a. What kind of $r$ value would she have been likely to find?

   b. Assume the computation resulted in an $r$ value of +.63. Write a verbal statement interpreting the results.

   c. What other variables might account for the variability in the exam scores that cannot be attributed to study time?

4. A study was conducted to determine the relationship between age and strength of handgrip. (Handgrip is measured by pounds of pressure placed on a mechanical device.)
    a. Sketch a scatterplot.
    b. Calculate the $r$ value for the following data.
    c. Comment on the shape of the scatterplot.

| Age | Handgrip |
|-----|----------|
| 4   | 5        |
| 7   | 8        |
| 13  | 11       |
| 18  | 22       |
| 29  | 24       |
| 38  | 24       |
| 47  | 23       |
| 58  | 21       |
| 67  | 17       |
| 76  | 13       |

## Post Test

1. What is the possible range of values for a correlation coefficient?

2. What is the meaning of an *r* value near 0?

3. Comment on the use of correlation to show cause and effect.

4. What is the meaning of an *r* value of +1.

5. The results of correlations for all possible pairs of variables in a given study can be shown in a _____ _____.

6. A relationship described with a curved line is called _____.

---

**Beyond the Basics**

Make an appointment to visit the counseling/testing center at your school. Ask if someone will review with you the examiner's manuals of any achievement, aptitude, or personality tests that they may have. Look for the section on test reliability and validity. Are there any studies reported in which correlation has been used to demonstrate reliability? What are the variables that were correlated? Is the correlation coefficient high enough to meet the standard for test reliability, $r = .80$ or higher?

# CHAPTER 10
# PREDICTION

## Learning Objectives

- Develop knowledge and understanding of the key terms.
- Calculate and interpret prediction intervals.

## Key Terms

**Least squares prediction equation**—The equation that minimizes the total of all squared prediction errors for known Y scores in the original correlation analysis.

**Standard error of prediction**—A rough measure of the average amount of predictive error.

**Squared correlation coefficient**—The proportion of the total variance in one variable that is predictable from its relationship with the other variable.

**Variance interpretation of $r^2$**—The proportion of variance explained by, or predictable from, the existing correlation.

## Text Review

By "predicting" what is known in a correlation of two variables, we can predict what is (1)_____. This is accomplished by placing a (2)_____ line in such a way that it passes through the main cluster of dots in the scatterplot. Positive and negative errors are avoided by squaring the difference between the predicted value and the actual value. Thus, the prediction line is referred to as the (3)_____ _____

_____ line or the (4)_____ _____
_____ line.

The search for the least squares prediction line would be a frustrating trial and error process, except for the precision of the least squares equation, (5)_____. In this equation, $Y'$ represents the (6)_____ value, and $X$ represents the (7)_____ value. The other values in the equation must be computed. When the computation is complete, the equation has the very desirable property of minimizing the total of all squared predictive errors for known values of $Y$ in the original correlation analysis. Note in the **Key Terms** section that this essentially defines the least squares prediction equation.

Two limitations exist for the application of the least squares prediction equation. One is that predictions may not be reliable if extended beyond the maximum value of $X$ in the original data. Second, since there is no proof of cause-effect in correlation, the desired effect simply may not occur.

Graphs may be constructed to depict the prediction equation. However, this should be done for (8)_____ purposes and not for prediction. It is more accurate to make the actual predictions from the (9)_____ _____ _____ _____.

The least squares prediction equation is designed to reduce error in prediction, but it does not eliminate it. Therefore, we must estimate the amount of error, understanding that the smaller the error, the more accurate our prediction. The estimated predictive error is expressed by the (10)_____ _____ _____ _____. This represents a rough measure of the average amount by which known $Y$ values deviate from their predicted $Y'$ values.

The value of $r$ is extremely important in relation to predictive error. When $r = 1$, the predictive error will be (11)_____. The most accurate predictions can be made when $r$ values represent (12)_____ relationships, whether positive or negative. Prediction should not be attempted when $r$ values are (13)_____, representing weak or nonexistent relationships.

There are some (14)_____ that must be met in order to apply the concepts of prediction we have been discussing. One is that using the prediction equation requires the underlying relationship to be (15)_____. Therefore, if the scatterplot for an original correlation analysis is (16)_____, this procedure would not be appropriate. A second assumption is that the dots in the original scatterplot will be dispersed equally about all segments of the prediction line. This is known as (17)_____. The third assumption is that for any given value of $X$, the corresponding distribution of $Y$ values is (18)_____ distributed. The final assumption is that the original data set of paired observations must be fairly large, usually in the hundreds.

The square of the (19)_____ _____, $r^2$, indicates the proportion of total variance in one variable that is predictable from its relationship with the other variable. In order to understand $r^2$ (the correlation coefficient squared), think for a moment about variability in a single distribution, which we studied in Chapter 5. In a single variable, we described variability with the measure of the standard deviation. We studied the variability graphically by looking at the shape of the frequency polygon. In a scatterplot, two variables are depicted graphically. Imagine a frequency polygon along the horizontal axis of the scatterplot. This shows the shape of the distribution for variable $X$. Imagine also a frequency polygon along the vertical axis of the scatterplot. This shows the shape of the distribution for variable $Y$. As we examine the relationship between the two variables, we know that some of the variability in Y must be due to the variability in $X$.

Let's substitute real data and think this through. Variable $X$ represents SAT scores. Variable Y represents college GPA. These variables constitute a strong positive relationship, approximately .57. There must be many reasons why GPA in college would vary. Some of that variability is probably due to preparation for college as reflected by SAT scores. The remaining variability might be due to such factors as whether the student works, how the adjustment is made to living away from home, and how many hours per week are devoted to studying or partying. The actual amount of variability in college GPA, variable $Y$, that can be explained by the variability in $X$, SAT scores, is reflected by the value of $r^2$. Thus we compute .57 squared = .3249, or .32. We interpret this value by saying that 32 percent of the variability of $Y$ can be explained by the variability in $X$. The remaining 68 percent of the variability of $Y$ would be explained by a combination of many other factors or variables, probably some of those mentioned earlier.

The value of $r^2$ supplies a direct measure of the (20)_____ of the relationship.

## Problems and Exercises

1. Recall the correlation problem from Chapter 9, examining the relationship between shooting a basketball ($X$) and pitching horseshoes ($Y$). Using a new set of data, a positive correlation of .85 was found. The means and standard deviations are as follows:

   $X = 8.75$    $Y = 7.75$

   $S_x = 2.12$    $S_y = 2.25$

   a. Determine the least squares equation for predicting number of ringers in horseshoes from number of baskets made in basketball.

   b. Calculate the standard error of prediction, $S_{y/x}$.

   c. Predict the number of horseshoe ringers made by Larry, who made eleven baskets out of the fifteen attempts.

   d. Predict the horseshoe pitching score for Earl, who scored only five baskets.

2. For more practice, return to Chapter 9 and change the values of $Y$ to create a lower positive correlation between horseshoe pitching and basketball. Then answer the preceding questions. Don't forget, you must calculate a new mean and standard deviation for $Y$, as well as the new correlation coefficient. The values for $X$ will remain the same.

## Post Test

Answer each of the following questions true or false.

_____ 1. When the value of $r$ equals either +1.00 or -1.00, the standard error must equal 0.

_____ 2. In a normal bivariate distribution, the mean of $Y$ will equal the mean of $X$.

_____ 3. When the value of $r$ increases, the standard error of the estimate decreases.

_____ 4. In a scatterplot, the predicted variable is usually on the $Y$ axis.

_____ 5. The standard error of estimate is a type of standard deviation.

_____ 6. The plotting of a regression line is not logical unless the value of $r$ differs significantly from 0.

_____ 7. The least squares prediction equation minimizes the total of all squared predictive errors for known $Y$ scores in the original correlation analysis.

_____ 8. The value of $1 - r^2$ indicates the proportion of variability in $Y$ that is predicted by $X$.

_____ 9. The value of $r^2$ can be interpreted as the proportion of explained variance.

_____ 10. Individual scores can be described by $r^2$.

---

**Beyond the Basics**
Discuss with one of your classmates some practical applications for prediction techniques in applied situations in such fields as education, business, medicine, and politics. You might also locate professional journals from the area that interests you most and try to find reports of research using prediction techniques. You will be pleased at your new ability to understand the statistical aspects as you read.

# CHAPTER 11
# POPULATIONS AND SAMPLES

## Learning Objectives

- Develop knowledge and understanding of key terms.

- Use the table of random numbers and the "fishbowl" method to select a random sample from a population.

- Understand and apply the concept of random assignment of subjects.

## Key Terms

**Population**—Any complete set of observations (or potential observations).

**Sample**—Any subset of observations from a population.

**Random sample**—A sample produced when all potential observations in the population have equal chances of being selected.

## Text Review

Populations may be (1)_____ or (2)_____. A real population is one in which all observations are (3)_____ at the time of sampling. A hypothetical population is one in which all observations are (4)_____ at the time of (5)_____. Often it is not convenient or even possible to include all observations in a research project. In such cases, a (6)_____ or subset of observations is taken. The size of the sample is partially determined by estimated (7)_____ among observations and by an acceptable amount of (8)_____.

In order to use inferential statistics, the analysis must be based on a

(9)_____ sample. A sample is random, if at each stage of the

sampling, the selection process guarantees that all remaining

(10)_____ have (11)_____ chances of

being selected.

The observations in a randomly selected sample should be

(12)_____ of those in the population. However, there

is no guarantee of this. The term random describes the process, and not

necessarily the outcome.

One of the best-known techniques for selecting a random sample is the

(13)_____ method. All observations must be

represented on slips of paper that are deposited in a bowl and

(14)_____. The thorough stirring is a very important

aspect of this method of sample selection.

Another method for generating a random sample involves the use of the table

of (15)_____ numbers. When using this table, the number of

digits actually used is determined by the (16)_____

_____. This method is not very efficient for obtaining a sample from a

(17)_____ population.

In an experiment, although subjects may not be selected randomly, they

should be randomly assigned to either the experimental or control condition.

The purpose of random assignment is to make sure that, except for

(18)_____ differences, groups of subjects are similar with

respect to any (19)_____ _____.

It is usually desirable that (20)_____ numbers of subjects be
assigned to the experimental and control groups. To accomplish this,
assignment should be done in (21)_____,

## Problems and Exercises

1. The state of Texas runs a lottery in which fifty numbered balls are dropped
   into a clear container and kept bouncing. Six of these fifty are then
   selected one at a time to represent the winning lottery numbers for that
   particular drawing.

   a. Does the lottery employ random sampling techniques?

   b. What is the significance of keeping the balls bouncing?

   c. Why is it necessary for the container to be clear?

2. One method to randomly assign subjects to either the experimental group
   or control group is to use a six-sided die. When the die is rolled, if an odd
   number appears, the subject is assigned to the experimental group, and if
   an even number is rolled, the subject is assigned to the control group.

   a. What should be done to ensure that the groups are equal in number?

   b. What would be another way of using the die to make the assignment
   of subjects to the two groups?

## Post Test

1. Describe the fishbowl method of selecting a random sample.

2. Define a random sample.

3. What is the purpose of random assignment in an experiment?

4. Differentiate between a real and a hypothetical population.

5. What components should be included in a rule for using the table of random numbers?

---

**Beyond the Basics**

Write a description of a population that you would be interested in studying. Did you describe a real population or a hypothetical one? Think about how you would select a sample from this population.

# CHAPTER 12
# PROBABILITY

## Learning Objectives

- Develop knowledge and understanding of key terms.

- Calculate and interpret probability problems.

## Key Terms

**Probability**—The proportion or fraction of times that a particular outcome is likely to occur.

**Independent outcomes**—The occurrence of one outcome has no effect on the probability that the other outcome will occur.

**Conditional probability**—Probability of one outcome, given the occurrence of another outcome.

**Addition rule**—Add together the separate probabilities of several mutually exclusive outcomes to find the probability that any one of these outcomes will occur.

**Multiplication rule**—Multiply together the separate probabilities of several independent outcomes to find the probability that these outcomes will occur together.

**Mutually exclusive outcomes**—Outcomes that cannot occur together.

## Text Review

(1)_____ refers to the proportion or fraction of times that a particular outcome will occur. Eventually, we will want to specify the probability of a particular outcome. Probability can be determined by (2)_____ or (3)_____. Probability values can vary between (4)_____ and (5)_____, and a set of probability values will always sum to (6)_____. Probabilities for various outcomes can be determined by the (7)_____ and (8)_____ rules. The addition of probabilities is appropriate when none of the outcomes can occur together. These are called (9)_____ _____ outcomes. They are usually connected by the word *or* and require the use of the addition rule. When outcomes are not mutually exclusive, don't forget to adjust the addition rule. When probability questions involve clusters of simple outcomes connected by the word *and*, apply the (10)_____ rule. This rule is appropriate because the occurrence of one outcome has no effect on the probability of the other outcome. Outcomes of this kind are called (11)_____. When the occurrence of one outcome does affect the probability of the other outcome, the probability of the second outcome must be adjusted to reflect this. The probability of one event, given the occurrence of another event, is referred to as (12) _____ probability. Areas under the theoretical normal curve can be interpreted as (13)_____.

Generally speaking, common outcomes are associated with a lack of

(14)_____ _____. On the other hand,

(15)_____ outcomes are associated with statistical significance.

## Problems and Exercises

1. Anagrams are formed by changing the order of letters in a word to make a new word. Listed below are the possible ways the letters of the word *tea* can be arranged.

   tea    tae    ate    aet    eat    eta

   a. If an anagram is chosen at random, what is the probability that it will be an English word, as opposed to a nonsense syllable?

   b. What is the probability that a randomly chosen letter arrangement will be either a word or a nonsense syllable?

   c. What probability rule did you use to solve part b?

   d. What is the probability of randomly choosing the word *eat*?

   e. What is the probability of randomly choosing either the word *eat* or the word *ate*?

2. A student takes a statistics exam that consists of multiple-choice items, each with four answer choices. She feels confident of her answers on all but four questions.

   a. What is the probability that she will guess correctly on all four that she doesn't know?

b. What is the probability that she will get all four of the questions wrong?

c. What could the instructor do, if anything, to decrease the probability of the student guessing correct answers?

3. Why do multiple-choice tests determine better than true-false tests which students really have knowledge of course material?

4. A man has socks in a drawer mixed at a ratio of four pairs of white ones to five pairs of black ones. How many single socks would he have to take out without knowing the color before he had a matching pair? Watch out. This is tricky.

## Post Test

1. What is the possible range of values of probabilities?

2. What is the sum of all probabilities in a set?

3. What rule should apply for probability problems when outcomes are mutually exclusive?

4.  When should the multiplication rule be used?

5.  What is the significance of the fact that probabilities represent area under the curve?

---

**Beyond the Basics**

Think about the odds or probability of winning in the various games of chance in gambling casinos. Which ones, if any, would most favor the patron? Which would be most representative of the theory of probability? Is there anything a would-be gambler could do (short of cheating of course) to be better prepared? You may want to find a book on gambling that would help you answer some of these questions.

Many states now have lotteries, gambling games based on extremely small probabilities of winning unusually large amounts of money, often millions of dollars. Find out if your state has a lottery and determine the probability of winning based on the purchase of one lottery ticket.

---

# CHAPTER 13
# SAMPLING DISTRIBUTION OF THE MEAN

## Learning Objectives

- Develop knowledge and understanding of the key terms.

- Understand the theoretical concepts of the sampling distribution of the mean.

## Key Terms

**Sampling distribution of the mean**—Probability distribution of means for all possible random samples of a given size from some population.

**Standard error of the mean**—Being the standard deviation of the sampling distribution of the mean, it's a rough measure of the average amount by which sample means deviate from the population mean.

**Central limit theorem**—A statement that the shape of the sampling distribution of the mean will approximate a normal curve if the sample size is sufficiently large.

## Text Review

A sampling distribution of means refers to the distribution that would exist if all possible samples of a given size were taken from some population and the mean of each of these samples was calculated. Then a distribution would be created from all these means, just as distributions have been created for sets of observations. A mean could be calculated for this distribution, and various observed sample means could be examined in light of distance from the mean of the sampling distribution. Thus, the sampling distribution allows us to determine whether a particular observed sample mean could be viewed as a common or rare outcome. If the observed sample mean is near the mean of the sampling distribution, then it would be a (1)_____ outcome. (Remember the characteristics of the standard normal curve from Chapter 6; 68 percent of the observed sample means would be within one standard deviation of the mean of the sampling distribution.) If the observed sample mean is very different from the mean of the sampling distribution, then it would be viewed as a (2)_____ outcome.

In reality, a sampling distribution is not constructed. Even with a computer, it would be a horrendous task. Instead, statistical theory supplies the information we need to understand the important idea of the sampling distribution. A highly simplified example of a sampling distribution is created in Section 13.2 of the text. You may wish to reread this section, carefully studying the accompanying figures and tables. From this example, we learn that all values of the sample mean do not occur with equal probability.

There are new symbols to learn which identify the mean and standard deviation of the sampling distribution and the population. The Greek letters $\mu$ (mu) and $\sigma$ (sigma) represent the (3)_____ and

(4)_____ _____ of any population.

The Greek letters $\mu_{\bar{x}}$ (mu, sub x, bar) and $\sigma_{\bar{x}}$ (sigma, sub x, bar) represent the

(5)_____ and the (6)_____

_____ of all sample means in a sampling distribution.

To avoid confusion, the sigma, sub x, bar term is usually referred to as the

(7)_____ _____ _____ _____

_____.

The sampling distribution of means has a mean, and this mean will always equal the (8)_____ mean. Therefore, the two terms may be used interchangeably in inferential statistics so that any claims made about the population mean apply to the mean of the sampling distribution and vice versa. Even when a distinction is made for the purpose of emphasis, it is important to note that the numerical value of the two is always the same.

The sampling distribution also has a standard deviation that is referred to as the (9)_____ _____ _____ _____ _____.
The standard error of the mean equals the (10)_____ _____ of the population divided by the square root of the (11)_____ _____. The standard error of the mean is a measure of (12)_____ in the sampling distribution. This variability decreases as sample size increases. Therefore, more precise generalizations may be made from samples to populations when sample size is (13)_____.

The central limit theorem states that the shape of the sampling distribution of the mean will approximate a normal curve if the sample size is sufficiently large. A sample size between (14)_____ and _____ is considered sufficiently large. The fact that the sampling distribution approximates the shape of a normal curve is important because it allows us to make statements about the sampling distribution by referring to the table for the standard normal curve.

Sampling distributions can be constructed for medians, proportions, standard deviations, and variances, as well as for other measures. Therefore, it is necessary to provide a full description and refer to the "sampling distribution of the mean" and never just the "sampling distribution."

# Problems and Exercises

## True or False

_____ 1. The standard deviation of a sampling distribution is the standard error of that distribution.

_____ 2. The population mean and the mean of the sampling distribution represent the same theoretical concept, but not the same numerical value.

_____ 3. As the sample size decreases, the standard error also decreases.

_____ 4. The sampling distribution of the mean is a theoretical concept and would not actually be constructed.

_____ 5. According to the central limit theorem, in order for the researcher to make the assumption of normality, the sample size must be between 25 and 100.

_____ 6. If a population distribution is skewed, a sampling distribution based on sample size of 50 will also be skewed.

_____ 7. The symbol $\mu$ represents the population mean.

_____ 8. The distribution for the population and the sampling distribution of the mean have in common the fact that one deals with all possible observations and the other with all possible random samples.

_____ 9. A sample differs in that it contains only a subset of the possible observations.

_____ 10. Any claims that can be made about the population mean can also be made about the sample mean.

_____ 11. Any claims about the population mean can also be made about the mean of the sampling distribution.

_____ 12. Random samples do not usually represent the underlying population exactly.

## Post Test

1. Match the following symbols with the appropriate measure.

   a. population mean $\qquad$ $\mu_{\bar{x}}$
   b. population standard deviation $\qquad$ $\mu$
   c. mean of the sampling distribution $\qquad$ $\sigma_{\bar{x}}$
   d. standard error of the mean $\qquad$ $\bar{X}$
   e. sample mean $\qquad$ $\sigma$

2. What is the relationship between sample size and variability in the sampling distribution?

3. Define the standard error of the mean.

4. What is the sample size needed to meet the central limit theorem?

5. Explain the relationship between the population mean and the mean of the sampling distribution.

---

**Beyond the Basics**

Many times students are tempted to skim lightly or ignore charts, graphs, and tables. In this chapter, these helpful visual aids can be a major factor in understanding the theoretical concept of the sampling distribution of the mean. Go back to your text and carefully study all the visual aids in Chapter 13. A true test of your understanding will be to attempt to explain some of the tables or figures to someone else. If you have not already organized a study group for this class, this would be a good time to do so. Keep the group small; three or four is ideal. Also, try to identify students who are about your same level of ability or understanding or higher. A study group composed entirely of people who are struggling in the course will not be very helpful.

# CHAPTER 14

# INTRODUCTION TO HYPOTHESIS TESTING: THE z TEST

## Learning Objectives

- Develop knowledge and understanding of the key terms.

- Calculate and interpret the $z$ test for a population mean.

- Determine appropriate level of significance for hypothesis tests, write alternate and null hypotheses, and formulate a decision rule.

- Determine appropriate use of one- and two-tailed tests.

## Key Terms

**Sampling distribution of $z$**—The distribution of $z$ values that would be obtained if a value of $z$ was calculated for each sample mean for all possible random samples of a given size from some population.

**Z Test for a population mean**—A hypothesis test that evaluates how far the observed sample mean deviates, in standard error units, from the hypothesized population mean.

**Null hypothesis $(H_0)$**—A statistical hypothesis that usually asserts that nothing special is happening with respect to some characteristic of the underlying population.

**Alternative hypothesis $(H_1)$**—The opposite of the null hypothesis.

**Research hypothesis**—Usually identified with the alternative hypothesis, this is the informal hypothesis or hunch that inspires the entire investigation.

**Decision rule**—Specifies precisely when $H_0$ should be rejected (because the observed $z$ qualifies as a rare outcome).

**Critical *z* score**—A *z* score that separates common from rare outcomes and hence dictates whether $H_0$ should be retained or rejected.

**Level of significance ($\alpha$)**—The degree of rarity required of an observed outcome in order to reject the null hypothesis ($H_0$).

## Text Review

A null hypothesis is tentatively assumed to be true. It is tested by determining whether an observed sample mean qualifies as a common outcome or a rare outcome in the hypothesized sampling distribution. An observed sample mean qualifies as a (1)_____ outcome if the difference between its value and that of the hypothesized population mean is small enough to be viewed as merely another random outcome. A common outcome signifies that nothing special is happening in the underlying population and thus the null hypothesis should be (2)_____. An observed sample mean qualifies as a (3)_____ outcome if the difference between its value and the hypothesized value is too large to be reasonably viewed as merely another random outcome. A rare outcome will be a mean that deviates so far from the hypothesized mean that it would emerge from the sparse concentration of possible sample means in either tail of the sampling distribution.

For the actual hypothesis test, it is customary to convert the mean to a (4)____ _____, the familiar standard score conversion presented in Chapter 6. This conversion yields a sampling distribution that approximates the (5)_____ _____ _____. The conversion is accomplished by the *z* score formula variation where *z* equals the observed sample mean minus the hypothesized population mean divided by the standard error.

The $z$ test is accurate only when (a) the population is normally distributed or the sample size is large enough to satisfy the requirements of the (6)_____ _____ theorem and (b) the population standard deviation is known.

The most crucial and exciting phase of the research is the formulation of the (7)_____ _____. The problem is then translated into the (8)_____ hypothesis, which asserts that nothing special is happening with respect to some characteristic of the underlying population. The null hypothesis always makes a precise statement about a number, never a range of numbers. This single number actually used in the null hypothesis may be based on available information about a relevant population, or it may be based on some existing standard or theory. The null hypothesis also always makes a statement about a characteristic of the (9)_____, never about a characteristic of the sample.

In general, the alternative hypothesis asserts the opposite of the (10)_____ hypothesis and it specifies a range of values about the single number that appears in the null hypothesis. The alternative hypothesis is usually identified with the (11)_____ hypothesis, the informal hypothesis or hunch that, by implying the presence of something special in the underlying population, serves as inspiration for the entire investigation.

A (12)_____ _____ specifies precisely when $H_0$ should be rejected. Decision rules are based on critical $z$ scores that separate common from rare outcomes and dictate whether $H_0$ should be retained or rejected. We can identify the proportion of the total area under the sampling distribution that is identified with rare outcomes. This proportion is often

83

referred to as (13)_____ _____ _____. The level of significance indicates the degree of rarity among random outcomes required to reject the null hypothesis. The null hypothesis is rejected if the observed $z$ value equals or exceeds the critical $z$ value because it deviates too far into the tails of the sampling distribution. After a decision has been made to retain or reject the null hypothesis, the decision must be (14)_____.

To summarize, the step-by-step procedure for testing a hypothesis is: (1) state the research problem, (2) identify the statistical hypotheses, (3) specify a decision rule, (4) calculate the value of the observed $z$, (5) make a decision, and (6) interpret the decision.

## Problems and Exercises

1. Assume that nationwide, the average age of nursing home residents is 76 years with a standard deviation of 3.5. A nursing home administrator in Texas wishes to determine whether the state average differs from the national average. Taking a random sample of 35 residents from nursing homes in Texas, he finds a mean age of 78. Using alpha = .05, test the null hypothesis. Be sure to write hypotheses, a decision rule, and an interpretation.

2. Average IQ is 100 with a standard deviation of 15. An educational diagnostician wishes to determine whether learning-disabled students in her school district exceed the mean IQ. (Note: One of the criteria for learning-disabled students is having IQ in the normal or above normal range.) She takes a random sample of 33 students and finds a mean IQ of 108. Using alpha = .05, test the null hypothesis. Be sure to write hypotheses, a decision rule, and an interpretation.

3. Assume that the national average composite score on the ACT is 18 with a standard deviation of 5. The B.A. Nurse RN school uses a cutoff score of 16 as admission criteria. The program administrator wants to determine whether the current students' averages are different from the national average of 18. A random sample of 42 currently enrolled students yields an average score of 20. Using alpha = .05, test the null hypothesis. Be sure to write hypotheses, a decision rule, and an interpretation.

## Post Test

1. Why are population means converted to $z$ for hypothesis testing?


2. What are the assumptions that must be met in order to use a $z$ test?


3. The _____ hypothesis supplies the value about which the hypothesized sampling distribution is centered.


4. The _____ _____ asserts the opposite of the null hypothesis.


5. The rejection of $H_0$ is precisely stated by the _____ _____.


6. The proportion of area under the curve that is identified with rare outcomes is referred to as _____ ____ _____.


7. List the steps in the procedure for testing a hypothesis.


---

**Beyond the Basics**
In the library, find a journal article that reports the results of a $z$ test. Determine whether the article format follows a structure similar to the one in your text for summarizing the hypotheses, the decision rule, critical $z$ scores, and interpretation. What is different? Was the sample size appropriate? Did the sample size satisfy the central limit theorem requirements?

# CHAPTER 15
# MORE ABOUT HYPOTHESIS TESTING

## Learning Objectives

- Develop knowledge and understanding of the key terms.

- Understand the important influence of sample size on hypothesis testing.

- Learn how to determine whether to use a one- or two-tailed hypothesis test.

- Learn to choose an appropriate level of significance.

## Key Terms

**Two-tailed or nondirectional test**—Rejection regions are located in both tails of the distribution.

**One-tailed or directional test**—Rejection region is located in just one tail of the distribution.

## Text Review

The importance of hypothesis tests is that they allow the researcher to

(1)_____ beyond existing data. In this process, the

(2)_____ _____ helps the researcher assess the effects

of chance. If the researcher rejects a true null hypothesis, he would make a

(3)_____ __ _____. It would be a (4)_____ __ error

if the researcher retains a false null hypothesis.

Retaining $H_0$ is viewed as a weak decision and rejecting $H_0$ is seen as a

(5)_____ decision. The decision to retain $H_0$ implies not that it is probably true, but that it could be true, whereas the decision to reject $H_o$ implies that it is probably false and that $H_1$ is probably true. This is not a serious problem, as most researchers ultimately hope to reject the null hypothesis.

The research hypothesis is not tested directly because it lacks the necessary precision. A hypothesis must specify a single number about which the sampling distribution can be constructed. The null hypothesis meets this requirement. Furthermore, because the research hypothesis is identified with the alternative hypothesis, the decision to reject the null hypothesis will provide strong support for the research hypothesis.

In a two-tailed or (6)_____ test, rejection regions are located in both tails of the sampling distribution, and the alternative hypothesis is concerned with a difference in the population mean in either direction. The difference could be either higher or lower. In a one-tailed or (7)_____ test, the rejection region is located in just one tail of the sampling distribution. Therefore, the observed sample mean triggers the decision to reject the null hypothesis only if it differs in the specified direction. Before the hypothesis test is conducted, the researcher must decide whether to conduct a one- or two-tailed test and which direction (if one-tailed) is significant. The (8)_____ test is extra-sensitive.

The level of significance must also be chosen before the hypothesis test is conducted. The level of significance equals the probability that even though the null hypothesis is true, an error could occur, and it could be rejected.

Therefore, when the rejection of a true null hypothesis would have serious consequences, a smaller level of significance would be appropriate. Alpha may be set to equal .01 or .001. The researcher chooses alpha and must do so before looking at the data.

## Problems and Exercises

1. What value in a hypothesis test reflects a consideration of the influence of chance?

2. Explain why the decision to retain the null hypothesis is considered weak.

3. List two reasons why the null hypothesis is tested rather than the research hypothesis.

4. Explain how the level of significance is determined for a hypothesis test.

5. Explain how the researcher determines whether to conduct a one-tailed or two-tailed test.

## Post Test

**True or False**

_____ 1. Having made a decision about the null hypothesis, we never really know if it is true or false.

_____ 2. A type I error consists of rejecting a true null hypothesis.

_____ 3. A type II error consists of retaining a true null hypothesis.

_____ 4. When generalizing beyond existing data, there is always the possibility of type I or type II errors.

_____ 5. Retaining the null hypothesis is considered a weak decision.

_____ 6. Most researchers hope to retain the null hypothesis.

_____ 7. Retaining the null hypothesis indicates that it is definitely true.

_____ 8. A one-tailed test is more sensitive than a two-tailed test.

_____ 9. The customary level of significance is .05.

_____ 10. A level of significance equal to .01 is the largest reported in professional journals.

---

**Beyond the Basics**

Describe a population that is of interest to you. Then try to think of a research problem. If conducting a hypothesis test, would you do a one- or two-tailed test? What level of significance would you use? Explain your answers or discuss these ideas with your instructor.

---

# CHAPTER 16
# CONTROLLING TYPE I AND TYPE II ERRORS

## Learning Objectives

- Develop knowledge and understanding of the key terms.
- Differentiate between type I and type II errors.
- Understand the important influence of sample size on hypothesis testing.

## Key Terms

**Type I error**—Rejecting a true null hypothesis.

**Type II error**—Retaining a false null hypothesis.

**Effect**—Any difference between a true and a hypothesized population mean.

**Hypothesized sampling distribution**—Centered about the hypothesized population mean, this distribution is used to generate the decision rule.

**True sampling distribution**—Centered about the true population mean, this distribution produces the one observed mean (or $z$).

**Alpha ($\alpha$)**—The probability of a type I error, that is, the probability of rejecting a true null hypothesis.

**Beta ($\beta$)**—The probability of a type II error, that is, the probability of retaining a false null hypothesis.

**Power ($1-\beta$)**—The probability of detecting a particular effect.

**Power curves**—Show how the likelihood of detecting any possible effect varies with different sample sizes.

## Text Review

When conducting a hypothesis test, there are four possible outcomes. Rejecting a false null hypothesis would constitute a (1)_____ _____. Retaining a (2)_____ null hypothesis would also be a correct decision. However, if the researcher rejects a true null hypothesis, he would make a (3)_____ __ _____. It would be a (4)_____ __ error if the researcher retains a false null hypothesis. The null hypothesis states that there is no (5)_____, contradicting the research hypothesis.

When $H_0$ is true, the hypothesized sampling distribution qualifies as the (6)_____ sampling distribution. However, when a randomly selected sample mean originates from the rejection region just by chance, then $H_0$ is rejected and the researcher has made a (7)_____ __ error. The probability of a type I error equals (8)_____. The probability of a correct decision equals (9)_____.

Type I errors are often called (10)_____ _____ because decisions may be made, money may be spent, or further research may be prompted when none of these is truly warranted.

When $H_0$ is false, an incorrect decision or type II error is called a (11)_____ because the effect goes undetected. The probability of a type II error is (12)_____. Whenever the effect is (13)_____, the probability of a correct decision is high and equals (14)_____. On the other hand, when the effect is (15)_____, the probability of a correct decision is lower and the probability of a type II error increases.

94

One way to increase the probability of detecting a false null hypothesis is to increase (16)_____ _____. This is true because increasing sample size causes a reduction in the (17)_____ _____. An extremely large sample size will thus produce a very sensitive hypothesis test. This is not always desirable because the test would detect even a small effect that has no practical importance.

The power of a hypothesis test equals the probability of detecting an (18) _____. To determine appropriate sample size, the researcher must decide (a) what is the smallest effect that merits detection and (b) what is an appropriate detection rate. When these two questions have been answered, the researcher determines sample size by consulting (19)_____ _____.

## Problems and Exercises

1. Before a hypothesis test, we are concerned about four possible outcomes. After a decision has been made to retain or reject the null hypothesis, we are concerned about only two possible outcomes. Explain.

2. A researcher reports that $H_0$ was rejected at the .05 level of significance for a hypothesis test using 250 subjects. Make suggestions as to how this research could be improved.

3. If $H_0$ is true, the probability of a type I error will always equal alpha. What is the probability of a correct decision?

4. If $H_0$ is false, the probability of a type II error is beta. What is the probability of a correct decision?

5. What can be done to increase the probability of detecting a false $H_0$?

6. What factor (that cannot be manipulated by the researcher) can increase the probability of a type II error or decrease the probability of a correct decision?

7. In the preceding question, why is effect described as a factor that the researcher cannot manipulate?

## Post Test

### True or False

_____ 1. If $H_0$ is true, it is a correct decision to retain $H_0$.

_____ 2. When generalizing beyond existing data, there is always the possibility of a type I or type II error.

_____ 3. If the null hypothesis is true, the probability of a type I error equals 1 − alpha.

_____ 4. If $H_0$ is false, the probability of a type II error is equal to beta.

_____ 5. The smaller the effect, the lower the probability of a type II error.

_____ 6. The probability of detecting a false null hypothesis can be increased by decreasing sample size.

_____ 7. A good way to determine appropriate sample size is to use a power curve.

_____ 8. A proper sample size is neither unduly small nor excessively large.

---

## Beyond the Basics

Find articles in the professional journals of a subject area that interests you. Perhaps there is some well-known research study in your field with which you are familiar and you would like to examine a report of that research. Once you have found several articles, examine each one closely for information concerning sample size and selection of subjects and consider the following questions. Does the sample size seem appropriate? In the discussion section, does the author note any problems related to sample size? Is the alpha level appropriate for the sample size? Would you have chosen subjects in the same way? Does the sample size influence the credibility of the research?

# CHAPTER 17
# ESTIMATION

## Learning Objectives

- Develop knowledge and understanding of the key terms.

- Understand the use of point estimates.

- Construct and interpret confidence intervals.

- Understand the effect of sample size on confidence intervals.

- Determine when to construct a confidence interval and when to conduct a hypothesis test.

- Understand the use of confidence intervals for population percents.

## Key Terms

**Point estimate**—A single value that represents some unknown population characteristic, such as the population mean.

**Confidence interval**—A range of values that, with a known degree of certainty, includes an unknown population characteristic, such as a population mean.

**Level of confidence**—The percent of time that a series of confidence intervals includes the unknown population characteristic, such as the population mean.

**Margin of error**—That which is added to and subtracted from some sample value, such as the sample proportion or sample mean, to obtain the limits of a confidence interval.

## Text Review

A researcher may wish to estimate the value of a population mean rather than test a hypothesis based on a population mean. Estimation is possible with the use of (1)_____ _____ and (2)_____ _____. A point estimate is a single value that represents some unknown (3)_____ characteristic. The problem with point estimates is that they tend to be (4)_____ because of (5)_____ _____. Therefore, the researcher uses a more accurate type of estimate, (6)_____ _____. A confidence interval is a range of values that, with a known degree of certainty, includes an unknown population characteristic, such as a (7)_____ _____.

To understand confidence intervals, you must be aware of three important properties of the sampling distribution of the mean. (a) The mean of the sampling distribution always equals the (8)_____ _____. (b) The standard error of the sampling distribution equals the population standard deviation divided by the square root of the (9)_____ _____. (c) The shape of the sampling distribution approximates a normal distribution if sample size satisfies the (10)_____ _____ _____.

A confidence interval can be constructed using formula 17.1, where a value of $z$ from the standard normal table is multiplied by the standard error and this value is both added to and subtracted from the mean. In order to use this formula, the (11)_____ _____

_____ must be known and sample size must be at least (12)_____.

In practice, only one confidence interval is actually constructed, and it is either (13)_____ or (14) _____. Although we never really know whether a particular confidence interval is true or false, we can be reasonably confident when the level of confidence is 95 percent or more. The level of confidence indicates the percent of time that a series of confidence intervals includes the unknown population characteristic such as the population mean. An increase in confidence level causes a wider confidence interval that is less (15)_____ unless it is offset by an increase in (16)_____ _____.

Although many different levels of confidence have been used, (17)_____ and (18)_____ are the most prevalent. Confidence intervals are more narrow or precise when standard error is smaller. Since standard error is reduced when sample size is increased, the larger the sample size, the more precise the confidence interval.

In the behavioral sciences, hypothesis tests have been preferred to confidence intervals. However, (19)_____ _____ are more informative because they indicate the size of the (20)_____. A hypothesis test is most appropriate when the major concern is whether or not an (21)_____ is present. Otherwise, a confidence interval could be used and should be considered when the null hypothesis is rejected.

Pollsters often apply the concept of confidence intervals to percent data to produce (22)_____ _____ _____. Pollsters also use very large sample sizes, in contrast to researchers who use much smaller sample sizes for their (23)_____.

## Problems and Exercises

1. In Chapter 14, problem 1, it was concluded that the average age of nursing home residents in Texas differs from the national average of 76. Given a standard deviation of 3 years and a sample mean of 79, for a random sample of 36 elderly persons, construct a 95 percent confidence interval for mean age and interpret the confidence interval.

2. Refer to Chapter 14, problem 2. The null hypothesis was rejected. Now the educational diagnostician wishes to construct a confidence interval. Using the information in this problem from Chapter 14, answer the following questions:

   a. What is the best estimate of the unknown mean IQ for the entire population of learning-disabled students in the local school district?

   b. Construct a 99 percent confidence interval for the unknown population mean.

   c. Interpret the confidence interval.

3. On the basis of a random sample of 200 teenage viewers, a television pollster decides to cancel an after-school program series, reporting with 95 percent confidence that only between 22 and 38 percent of the potential viewing audience have been watching the series.

    a.  Comment on the width of the confidence interval.

    b.  What could be done to make the confidence interval more precise?

## Post Test

1. What are some of the similarities between hypothesis tests and confidence intervals?

2. Why are larger samples more acceptable in polls and surveys than in experiments?

3. What three properties of sampling distributions are essential to the understanding of confidence intervals?

4. What assumptions must be met in order to use formula 17.1 in constructing confidence intervals?

5. What is the relationship between sample size, standard error, and confidence intervals?

6. What is the difference between a point estimate and a confidence interval?




7. What is the disadvantage of using point estimates?




**Beyond the Basics**
Think about the logic a researcher would apply in deciding whether to construct a 95 or 99 percent confidence interval. Essentially the decision is based on the magnitude of the consequences of making an error. Find two research reports in professional journals, one reporting a 95 percent confidence interval and one reporting a 99 percent confidence interval. Do you agree with the researcher's judgment in each case? What is there about the research that makes a false interval more critical?

# CHAPTER 18

# *t* TEST FOR ONE SAMPLE

## Learning Objectives

- Develop knowledge and understanding of the key terms.

- Identify research problems appropriate for the use of the *t* test for one sample.

- Write hypotheses, solve for *t*, make correct decisions about the null hypothesis, and interpret the results of *t* tests.

## Key Terms

**Sampling distribution of *t*—**The distribution of *t* values that would be obtained if a value of *t* were calculated for each sample mean for all possible random samples of a given size from some population.

**Sample standard deviation—**The version of the sample standard deviation, with $n - 1$ in its denominator, that is used in statistical inference to estimate the unknown population standard deviation.

**Estimated standard error of the mean—**The version of the standard error of the mean that is used whenever the unknown population standard deviation must be estimated.

***t* ratio—**A replacement for the *z* ratio whenever the unknown population standard deviation must be estimated.

**Degrees of freedom—**The number of values free to vary, given one or more mathematical restrictions on a sample of observed values used to estimate some unknown population characteristic.

## Text Review

The sampling distribution of *t* was discovered by (1)_____

_____. In reality, there is a family of t distributions, each

associated with a number referred to as (2)_____ _____

_____. In the present case, the number of degrees of

freedom (df) always equals (3) ___ ____ ___ ___.

All *t* distributions are similar to *z* distributions in that they are symmetrical,

unimodal, and bell shaped. The biggest difference between *t* and *z*

distributions is the (4)_____ _____ of the *t*

distribution.

Tables for *t* distributions contain only the values that correspond to the

common levels of significance. The *t* values listed in the table are

(5)_____ and originate from the (6)_____ half of

the distribution. The symmetry allows the critical *t* values for the lower half of

the distribution to be obtained by simply placing a negative sign in front of

any table entry.

The *t* distribution has greater variability than the *z* distribution. This increased

variability arises from the estimated standard error of the mean and the chance

differences that could occur in the estimates. The extra variability also

explains the inflated tails of the curve in the *t* distribution. Because of this

extra variability, one could expect actual critical *t* values to be

(7)_____ than critical *z* values.

All hypothesis tests represent variations on a common theme. If some

observed characteristic, such as the mean for a random sample, qualifies as a

rare outcome under the null hypothesis, the hypothesis will be
(8)_____. Otherwise, the hypothesis will be
(9)_____. To determine whether an outcome is rare, the
observed characteristic is converted to a new value, such as $t$, and compared to
critical values from the appropriate sampling distribution.

To construct confidence intervals for estimating the population mean based on
a $t$ distribution, use the formula for confidence intervals previously presented
and substitute $t$ for $z$. The symmetrical limits of a confidence interval require
specifications like those of a two-tailed hypothesis test.

Use of the $t$ test requires some basic assumptions. Use $t$ rather than $z$ when the
(10)_____ _____ _____
is unknown. Assume that the underlying population is
(11)_____ _____. If the assumption of
normality is violated, the accuracy of the test is relatively unaffected as long
as (12)_____ _____ is sufficient.

Since the population standard deviation is unknown, it must be estimated. The
old formula for calculating standard deviation was appropriate for
(13)_____ statistics but not (14)_____.
The population standard deviation can be estimated from the sample standard
deviation by replacing $n$ with (15)_____ in the denominator. When
the unknown population standard deviation must be estimated, the population
standard error of the mean must also be estimated. The shift to this estimate
requires that the $z$ test be changed to $t$, where each distribution has its own
degrees of freedom.

(16)_____ _____ _____ refers to the number of values that are free to vary, given one or more mathematical restrictions on the entire set of values. The mathematical restriction relevant to degrees of freedom in *t* distributions is that the sum of all values, expressed as deviations from their mean, always equals (17)_____.

# Problems and Exercises

1. A psychology professor believes that his summer school class grades exceed the class average of 70 usually earned by students in the fall and spring semesters. A random sample of summer student grades yields the following results: 88, 72, 84, 77, 96, 67, 65.

   a. Test the null hypothesis with $t$ using the .05 level of significance.
   b. Construct a 95 percent confidence interval for the true grade average.
   c. Interpret the confidence interval.

2. Find the critical $t$ values for the following hypothesis tests:

    a.  Two-tailed test, $a = .001$, $df = 30$

    b.  One-tailed test, upper tail critical, $a = .01$, $df = 21$

    c.  One-tailed test, lower tail critical, $a = .05$, $df = 8$

3. Now assume a researcher made an error in choosing the appropriate hypothesis test and used $z$ instead of $t$ in the hypothesis tests in problem 2.

    a.  Find the critical $z$ value for each test.

    b.  How do the values differ?

    c.  What causes the differences?

4. Behavioral psychologists have established that a fixed ratio reinforcement schedule produces the highest rate of response. Upon learning this, a manufacturer of jeans decides to apply the principle in one of the factories on a trial basis. Before the trial, the average seamstress sewed 21 pockets per hour and was being paid by the hour. During the trial period, seamstresses were paid by the number of pockets completed (a fixed ratio reinforcement). The following results were obtained for a random sample of seamstresses: 18, 25, 28, 20, 31, 29, 24.

   a. Test the null hypothesis with $t$, using the .05 level of significance.
   b. Construct a 95 percent confidence interval for the true average number of pockets sewn in one hour.
   c. Interpret the confidence interval.
   d. If you owned stock in this company, would you favor the use of a fixed ratio reinforcement schedule to pay employees? Explain why.

## Post Test

1. What determines whether a *t* test or *z* test should be used?

2. How do critical values of *t* compare with critical values of *z*?

3. What are the assumptions that must be met for the proper use of a *t* test?

4. What happens to the *t* test if the assumption of normality is violated?

5. Define degrees of freedom.

---

**Beyond the Basics**

In this section in Chapter 14, you were asked to find a journal article reporting a *z* test. If you did this, using the data in that article, pretend that a *t* test is appropriate and compare the appropriate critical *t* value to the critical *z*. Would the decision to reject or retain the null hypothesis be the same? Does the role of sample size change at all? If so, how? If you did not find an article for the assignment in Chapter 14, you may now find one reporting either *z* or *t*. Then answer the preceding questions comparing the results against a critical value for both *t* and *z*.

---

# CHAPTER 19
# *t* TEST FOR TWO INDEPENDENT SAMPLES

## Learning Objectives

- Develop knowledge and understanding of the key terms.

- Identify research problems appropriate for the use of the *t* test for two independent samples.

- Write hypotheses, solve for *t*, make correct decisions about the null hypothesis, and interpret the results of *t* tests for two independent samples.

## Key Terms

**Two independent samples**—Observations in one sample are not paired, on a one-to-one basis, with observations in the other sample.

**Sampling distribution of $\bar{X}_1 - \bar{X}_2$**—Differences between sample means based on all possible pairs of random samples—of given sizes—from two underlying populations.

**Effect**—Any difference between two population means.

**Standard error of $\bar{X}_1 - \bar{X}_2$**—A rough measure of the average amount by which any difference between sample means deviates from the difference between population means.

**Pooled variance estimate $(s^2_p)$**—The most accurate estimate of the population variance (assumed to be the same for both populations) based on a combination of two sample variances.

**Confidence interval for $\mu_1 - \mu_2$**—A range of values that, in the long run, includes the unknown difference between population means a certain percent of the time.

## Text Review

Two independent samples occur when (1)_____ in one sample are not paired with observations in the other sample. When a *t* test is conducted for two independent samples, the difference between population means reflects the (2)_____ of the variable being studied. In the example in the text, the variable is (3)_____ _____. When there is little difference between the two population means, there is little effect.

The null hypothesis states there is (4)_____ difference between population means. There are three possible alternative hypotheses. One states that the difference between population means doesn't equal zero. This would represent a (5)_____ test. A second possible hypothesis states that the difference is less than zero. This is a one-tailed test with the (6)_____ tail critical. The third possibility is a one-tailed test with (7)_____ tail critical which states that the difference between population means (8)_____ zero. When there is concern only about differences in a particular direction, a (9)_____ or one-tailed hypothesis test should be used.

Just as the sampling distribution of the mean (presented in Chapter 13) is not actually constructed, the sampling distribution for the difference between sample means is not constructed. Instead, we rely on statistical theory to provide information about the mean and standard error for the sampling distribution of $\bar{X}_1 - \bar{X}_2$. In practice, there is only one observed difference and the (10)_____ _____ is conducted to determine whether it qualifies as a common or rare outcome. In the one-sample case, the mean of the sampling distribution equals the mean of the (11)_____. In the two-sample case, the mean of the sampling distribution equals the (12)_____ between population means.

The sampling distribution of $\bar{X}_1 - \bar{X}_2$ has a standard deviation referred to as the (13)_____ _____ of the difference between sample means. The standard error is a rough measure of the average amount by which any difference between sample means deviates from the difference between (14)_____ _____. The size of the standard error decreases as sample size (15) _____.

Before the $t$ ratio can be calculated, the standard error must be estimated.

The $t$ test assumes that the two population variances are (16)_____.

A confidence interval may be constructed for the difference between population means. The confidence interval is a range of values that, in the long run, includes the unknown difference between population means a certain percent of the time. If both positive and negative values appear in a confidence interval, no single interpretation is possible. The inclusion of a zero value in the range indicates that the variable being studied may have (17)_____ _____.

The $t$ test for two independent samples assumes that both underlying populations are (18)_____ _____ and have (19)_____ variances. If sample sizes are (20)_____ _____ and _____, violations of these assumptions will be of little concern.

115

The pooled variance estimate can be obtained by combining the variance common to both populations. The pooled variance estimate is the most accurate estimate of the variance (assumed to be the same for both populations) based on a combination of the two sample variances. The degrees of freedom for the pooled variance estimate equal the sum of the two sample sizes minus two. Two degrees of freedom are lost because the (21)_____ in each of the two samples are expressed as (22)_____ from their respective sample means.

## Problems and Exercises

1. A researcher wishes to determine the effect of listening to music on memory of word lists. Twelve student volunteers are randomly assigned to two groups—one group listens to music while studying the word list $(X_1)$ and one group does not $(X_2)$. The mean performance on the test of memory for $X_1$ is 18 and the mean for $X_2$ is 23. The estimated standard error equals 1.45. Use $t$ to test the null hypothesis at the .05 level of significance.

2. A social psychologist wishes to determine the effect of fear on affiliation. Eighteen volunteers are randomly assigned to either a frightening description of an experiment or a non-frightening description. Then the volunteers respond to a questionnaire as to their preference for waiting while the experiment is prepared. Higher scores indicate more desire for affiliation or waiting with another volunteer. Lower scores indicate a preference for waiting alone. Using $t$, test the null hypothesis at the .01 level of significance.

### Affiliation Scores

| Frightened | Not Frightened |
|:---:|:---:|
| 18 | 12 |
| 15 | 6 |
| 17 | 8 |
| 13 | 13 |
| 15 | 12 |
| 19 | 6 |
| 22 | 10 |
| 19 | 7 |
| 20 | 11 |

## Post Test

1. List two important properties of the sampling distribution of the difference between sample means.

2. What are the appropriate degrees of freedom for the $t$ distribution for two independent samples?

3. When does the confidence interval for the difference between population means have a single interpretation?

4. What are the assumptions for the use of a $t$ test for independent samples?

---

**Beyond the Basics**

Make up your own research problem for a $t$ test for two independent samples. Write it up as a problem so that your fellow students can find the solution. Then work out a solution following the format in Table 19.1 in your text.

# CHAPTER 20
# *t* TEST FOR TWO MATCHED SAMPLES

## Learning Objectives

- Develop knowledge and understanding of the key terms.

- Identify research problems appropriate for the use of the *t* test for two matched samples.

- Write hypotheses, solve for *t*, make correct decisions about the null hypothesis, and interpret the results of *t* tests for two matched samples.

- Understand how to make decisions about matching research subjects.

- Understand the use of the repeated measures research design.

- Calculate and interpret *t* test for population correlation coefficient.

## Key Terms

**Two matched samples**—Each observation in one sample is paired, on a one-to-one basis, with a single observation in the other sample.

**Difference score**—The arithmetic difference between each pair of scores in two matched samples.

**Repeated measures**—Whenever the same subject is measured more than once.

**Counterbalancing**—Reversing the order of conditions for equal numbers of all subjects.

## Text Review

Two matched samples occur when each observation in one sample is
(1)_____ with a single observation in the other sample. The $t$
test for dependent samples involves using the difference score. This converts
the two-sample problem to a (2)_____-_____
problem. Thus, the original pair of populations becomes a single population of
(3)_____ _____. If the variable being
tested has no effect, then the population mean of all difference scores should
equal (4)_____.

A directional hypothesis with upper tail critical would state that the mean
difference (5)_____ zero. A directional hypothesis with
lower tail critical would state that the mean difference is
(6)_____ than zero. A nondirectional hypothesis simply states
that the mean difference is different from or not equal to zero. The mean of
the sampling distribution of $D$ equals the difference between population
means.

Degrees of freedom are different for the $t$ test for two matched samples
because $n$ equals the number of (7) _____ _____ and
not the number of observations.

One advantage of matching is that it eliminates one source of
(8)_____. Confidence intervals are interpreted much the
same for matched samples as for independent samples.

Matching is desirable only when some uncontrolled variable appears to have a
considerable impact on the variable being measured. Appropriate matching

reduces (9)_____ and the estimated (10)_____

_____. Therefore, matching (11)_____ the

sensitivity of the hypothesis test. To identify a variable that should be

matched, the researcher should be familiar with all previous research in the

area and conduct (12)_____ _____.

A test could involve the use of the same subjects in both samples. This is

referred to as (13)_____ _____.

A big advantage of repeated measures is that uncontrolled variability due to

individual differences is eliminated. This advantage may be offset by other

concerns, such as fatigue, practice, or motivation when subjects must perform

twice.

When subjects must perform in both conditions, it is customary to use

(14)_____, reversing the order of the

conditions for an equal number of all subjects.

The present $t$ test assumes that the population of difference scores is normally

distributed. Violations of this assumption will not matter much as long as

(15)_____ _____ is sufficiently large.

When the researcher wishes to determine whether there is a relationship

between two variables, the appropriate measure is the $t$ test for the population

correlation coefficient. The degrees of freedom are $n - 2$. Two degrees of

freedom are lost, one for variable $X$ and one for variable $Y$. In the $t$ test for

population correlation coefficient, sample size must be sufficiently large to

minimize sampling variability. In using this test, the researcher must assume

that the sample originates from a normal (16)_____

population.

## Problems and Exercises

1. A random sample of 45 applicants for a Master's program in clinical psychology reveals an *r* of .53 between their Graduate Record Exam scores and their grade point average in the course work. Test the null hypothesis with *t*, using the .05 level of significance.

2. An investigator wants to examine the effects of alcohol consumption on the number of errors made on a measure of manual dexterity. Four of the volunteers are tested first without alcohol, $X_1$, and then re-tested after consuming two drinks, $X_2$. The other five are tested in the reverse order with time allowed for the alcohol effects to wear off. Their performance is indicated in the following table.

**Number of Errors on Manual Dexterity**

| Subject | $X_1$ | $X_2$ |
|---------|-------|-------|
| 1 | 2 | 6 |
| 2 | 1 | 4 |
| 3 | 4 | 5 |
| 4 | 3 | 7 |
| 5 | 1 | 5 |
| 6 | 2 | 5 |
| 7 | 3 | 6 |
| 8 | 3 | 8 |
| 9 | 2 | 4 |

a. Using $t$, test the null hypothesis at the .05 level of significance.
b. Specify the $p$-value for the test result.

3. Assume the data in the following table were observed from an actual study represented by the following problem. A researcher wishes to determine whether attendance at a day care center increases the scores of three-year-old children on a motor skills test. Random assignment dictates which member from each of 10 pairs of twins attends the day care center and which member stays at home.

### Effect of Day Care on Motor Skills

| Pair No. | Day-care | At Home |
|----------|----------|---------|
| 1 | 23 | 20 |
| 2 | 19 | 16 |
| 3 | 17 | 18 |
| 4 | 25 | 20 |
| 5 | 22 | 19 |
| 6 | 24 | 18 |
| 7 | 21 | 20 |
| 8 | 18 | 18 |
| 9 | 20 | 17 |
| 10 | 25 | 19 |

a. Using $t$, test the null hypothesis at the .05 level of significance.
b. Specify the $p$-value for the test result.
c. What makes the samples dependent?
d. What are the variables important to control? How does the design of the experiment control them?

## Post Test

1. What significant transformation takes place with the use of difference scores?

2. What is a major difference between the sampling distribution for the difference scores and the sampling distribution for independent samples?

3. What are the appropriate degrees of freedom for the $t$ distribution of two matched samples?

4. What are the disadvantages of matching?

5. What are the advantages of matching?

6. When is matching appropriate?

7. What is repeated measures?

8. What are the assumptions for the *t* test for matched samples?

9. What happens if the assumption is violated?

10. What are the assumptions for using the *t* test for correlation coefficients?

---

**Beyond the Basics**

Make up your own research problem for a *t* test for two matched samples. Write it up as a problem so that your fellow students could find the solution. Then work out a solution following the format in your text. Compare the make-up of the samples used in this problem with the samples you created for this section in Chapter 19. How are matched samples different from independent samples? Would it be appropriate to use the same research question you used previously and alter the samples? Why or why not?

---

# CHAPTER 21

# BEYOND HYPOTHESIS TESTS: *p*-VALUES AND EFFECT SIZE

## Learning Objectives

- Develop knowledge and understanding of the key terms.

- Find *p*-values using the various statistical tables.

- Read and interpret *p*-values in research reports.

- Distinguish between *p*-values and level of significance.

- Distinguish between statistical significance and practical importance.

- Understand the use and interpretation of the squared point biserial correlation.

## Key Terms

**p-value**—The degree of rarity of a test result, given that the null hypothesis is true.

**Statistical significance**—Not an indication of importance; but merely that the null hypothesis is probably false.

**Effect**—Difference between population means.

**Squared point biserial correlation**—The proportion of variance in the dependent variable that can be explained by the independent variable.

## Text Review

If the researcher does not retain or reject the null hypothesis, but views it with suspicion, depending on the degree of rarity of the test result, then (1)_____ _____ are being used. Smaller $p$-values tend to discredit the null hypothesis and support the research hypothesis. Using $p$-values is a less structured approach to hypothesis testing.

If level of significance is set at .05, any $p$-value less than .05 implies that the null hypothesis would have been (2)_____ and any $p$-value greater than .05 implies that the null hypothesis would be (3)_____.

Computer generated $p$-values are more precise, but are interpreted in the same way as those read from the tables in the appendix of the text.

Using the less structured approach of (4)____-_____ allows the researcher to postpone a decision until subsequent investigations can provide further evidence. This is an attractive option when test results are (5)_____.

One disadvantage of this approach is that when a firm decision is not being made to retain or reject the null hypothesis, it is difficult to deal with the concepts of type I and (6)_____ _____ errors.

Results of hypotheses tests are often described as having statistical significance if the (7)_____ hypothesis has been rejected. Statistical significance indicates that the null hypothesis is probably false, but doesn't indicate whether it is seriously false or mildly false. Statistical significance may lack practical importance because sample size is (8)_____

_____.

One way to judge practical importance when large sample sizes are present is to use the squared (9)_____ _____ correlation. The squared point biserial correlation indicates the proportion of variance in the dependent variable that is predictable from the (10)_____ variable. Cohen suggested a rule of thumb for interpreting the values of squared point biserial correlations in relation to effect size. However, it is best not to apply any rule of thumb without considering special circumstances that could make even a very small effect very important.

## Problems and Exercises

1. You solved the problem below in Chapter 19. The observed $t$ value was 3.45.
   A researcher wishes to determine the effect of listening to music on memory of word lists. Twelve student volunteers are randomly assigned to two groups—one group listens to music while studying the word list $(X_1)$ and one group does not $(X_2)$. The mean performance on the test of memory for $X_1$ is 18 and the mean for $X_2$ is 23. The estimated standard error equals 1.45.

   a. Find the $p$-value for this value of $t$. (Hint: $df=10$)

   b. Would you reject the null hypothesis at the .01 level? At the .001 level?

2. Which of the following p-values would cause you to reject the null hypothesis at the .01 level.
   a. $p = .01$
   b. $p > .01$
   c. $p < .01$
   d. $p < .001$

3. You might read the following statement in a published research report. There is a statistically significant difference between the mean endurance scores in favor of blood-doped athletes $\{t(8) = 3.20, p < .01\}$.

   a. Given this result, what possible alpha level(s) could the researcher have used?
   b. Would the statement change if the alpha level had been set at .001?

4. Given a $t$ value of 2.12, and a sample size of 240 randomly assigned to two groups, calculate the value of the squared point biserial correlation coefficient. (Use formula 21.1.)

   a. Using Cohen's rule of thumb, how would you describe the effect size.

   b. Comment on the practical importance of this effect.

# Post Test

## True or False

_____ 1. The *p*-value of a test result represents the degree of rarity of that test result given that the null hypothesis is false.

_____ 2. Large *p*-values tend to support the null hypothesis.

_____ 3. Exact *p*-values listed on computer printouts would be interpreted exactly the same as those read from tables.

_____ 4. One advantage of the use of *p*-values is that the researcher may postpone a decision.

_____ 5. *P*-values and level of significance are essentially the same thing.

_____ 6. *P*-values may be used to determine whether the null hypothesis should be rejected.

_____ 7. Statistical significance indicates that the null hypothesis is definitely true.

_____ 8. Statistical significance that lacks practical importance is associated with small sample sizes.

_____ 9. The Pearson correlation can be used to determine practical importance in a test result.

_____ 10. Although Cohen's rule of thumb for interpreting squared point biserial correlations is helpful, special circumstances may render it irrelevant.

---

## Beyond the Basics

Look back at some of the research articles you have gathered, focusing on the *p*-values and the issue of sample size. Does the *p*-value appear in a statement similar to the examples in your text? Can you determine from the *p*-value whether the null hypothesis should be retained or rejected? What is the sample size? If supplied enough information, calculate the squared point biserial correlation and apply Cohen's rule of thumb. Then read the discussion section of the research. Do the researchers imply that an important effect has been found or merely that the effect has statistical significance?

# CHAPTER 22

# ANALYSIS OF VARIANCE (ONE WAY)

## Learning Objectives

- Develop knowledge and understanding of the key terms.

- Identify research problems appropriate for use of ANOVA.

- Write hypotheses, solve for $F$, make correct decisions about the null hypothesis, and interpret the results of $F$ tests for one-way ANOVA.

- Identify the appropriate situations for use of Scheffe's test and be able to interpret the results.

## Key Terms

**Analysis of variance (ANOVA)**—An overall test of the null hypothesis for more than two population means.

**One-way ANOVA**—The simplest type of analysis of variance that tests whether differences exist among population means categorized by only one factor or independent variable.

**Treatment effect**—The existence of at least one difference between the population means categorized by the independent variable.

**Variability between groups**—Variability among scores of subjects who, being in different groups, receive different experimental treatments.

**Variability within groups**—Variability among scores of subjects who, being in the same group, receive the same experimental treatment.

**Random error**—The combined effects (on the score of individual subjects) of all uncontrolled factors.

**Sum of squares (SS)**—The sum of the squared deviations of some set of scores about their mean.

**Degrees of freedom (df)**—The number of deviations free to vary in any sum of square term.

**Mean Square (*MS*)**—A variance estimate obtained by dividing a sum of squares by its degrees of freedom.

***F* ratio**—Ratio of the between-group mean square (for subjects treated differently) to the within-group mean square (for subjects treated similarly.)

**Squared curvilinear correlation**—The proportion of variance in the dependent variable that can be explained by the independent variable.

**Multiple comparisons**—The series of possible comparisons whenever more than two population means are involved.

**Scheffe's test**—A multiple comparison test that, regardless of the number of comparisons, never permits the cumulative probability of at least one type I error to exceed the specified level of significance.

## Text Review

Testing the null hypothesis for more than two population means requires a statistical procedure known as (1) _____ _____ _____.

Specifically, Chapter 22 deals with (2)_____ ANOVA, where population means differ with respect to only one factor. One source of variability in ANOVA is the differences between group means. Small differences can be attributed to (3)_____. However, relatively large differences between group means probably indicate that the null hypothesis is (4)_____. If there is at least one difference between the population means, there is (5)_____

_____. A second source of variability in ANOVA is an estimate of the variability within groups (subjects treated similarly). To make a decision about the null hypothesis, these two sources of variability are compared. The more that the variability between groups exceeds the variability within groups, the more likely the null hypothesis will be false. Regardless of whether the null hypothesis is true or false, the variability within groups reflects only (6)_____ _____.

Random error is the combined effects of all uncontrolled factors such as individual differences among subjects, variations in experimental conditions, and measurement errors. The within-group variability estimate is often referred to as the (7)_____ _____.

For three or more samples, the null hypothesis is tested with the $F$ ratio, variability between groups divided by variability within groups. $F$ has its own family of sampling distributions, so an $F$ table must be consulted to find the critical $F$ value. In the $F$ test, if the variability between groups sufficiently exceeds the variability within groups, then the null hypothesis will be rejected. If the null hypothesis is true, then the two estimates of variability (between and within groups) will reflect only random error. The values will be similar, so the $F$ will be small and the null hypothesis will be retained.

Variance is a measure of (8)_____. A variance estimate indicates that information from a sample is used to determine the unknown variance for a population. In ANOVA, a variance estimate is composed of the numerator, the sum of squares, and the denominator, which is always (9)_____ _____ _____.

When the ratio is calculated, it produces the mean of the squared deviations referred to as (10)_____ _____.

In ANOVA, most of the computational effort is in finding the various sum of squared terms. $SS_{between}$ equals the sum of the squared deviations of group means about their mean, the overall mean. $SS_{within}$ equals the sum of the squared deviations of all scores about their respective group means. $SS_{total}$ equals the sum of the squared deviations of all scores about the overall mean. Calculations of the sum of squares terms can be verified by calculating all

134

three from scratch and then checking because the sum of squares total equals the sum of squares within and the sum of squares between added together. For each sum of squares term, degrees of freedom differ. In ANOVA, the degrees of freedom for sum of squares total always equals the combined degrees of freedom for the other sum of squares terms.

Mean squares between reflects the variability between groups who are treated (11)_____. Mean squares within reflects the variability among scores for subjects who are treated (12)_____. Mean squares within measures only (13)_____ _____, but mean squares between measures (14)_____ _____. The observed $F$, once calculated, may be compared with the critical $F$ specified by the pair of degrees of freedom associated with it. Rejection of the null hypothesis indicates only that not all population means are equal.

The assumptions for the $F$ test are the same as for $t$. All underlying populations are assumed to be (15)_____ _____ with equal variances. Violations of the assumptions are not critical as long as sample size is greater than (16)_____. ANOVA techniques used in the text presume that scores are independent. Furthermore, attention should be paid to sample size so that it is not unduly small or excessively large.

Whenever a statistically significant $F$ has been obtained, the researcher should consider using the squared curvilinear correlation, $n^2$, and Cohen's rule of thumb to estimate (17)_____ _____ independently of sample size.

135

In order to pinpoint the one or more differences between pairs of population means that contribute to the rejection, a test of (18)_____ _____ must be used. Multiple $t$ tests cannot be used because it would increase the probability of a (19)_____ ____ error. Once the overall null hypothesis has been rejected in ANOVA, Scheffe's test can be used for all possible comparisons without the probability of the type I error exceeding the (20)_____ _____ _____. When sample sizes are unequal, Scheffe's critical value must be calculated for each comparison. But when sample sizes are equal, the critical mean difference is only calculated once and then used to evaluate the remaining comparisons. It is important to note that Scheffe's test should be used only when the overall null hypothesis has been rejected.

The $F$ test in ANOVA is equivalent to a (21)_____ test even though the rejection region appears only in the upper tail of the distribution. This is due to the squaring of all the values that makes it impossible to have a negative value for $F$.

## Problems and Exercises

1. The principal of an elementary school wishes to determine the most effective method to improve reading as measured by the district's reading achievement test. Twenty-eight children in third grade are randomly assigned to one of three reading improvement programs. Test the difference between their September reading scores and April reading scores using ANOVA to determine whether any one method is superior. Use the .05 level of significance. The difference scores follow.

   * Don't forget the Scheffe's test if appropriate.

   | Tutoring | Home Help | Reading Aloud |
   |----------|-----------|---------------|
   | 10 | 8 | 6 |
   | 7 | 6 | 9 |
   | 12 | 4 | 5 |
   | 9 | 4 | 7 |
   | 13 | 9 | 7 |
   | 11 | 7 | 6 |
   | 10 | 8 | 8 |
   | 14 | 5 | 5 |
   | 11 | 7 | 9 |
   |  | 8 |  |

2. A medical researcher wishes to identify the best method for reducing blood pressure. Thirty-eight volunteers with high blood pressure are randomly assigned to each of four groups. After four months of observation and treatment, the following results are obtained. Results represent the difference in blood pressure before and after treatment. Using the $F$ test, .05 level of significance, test the null hypothesis. Use Scheffe's test if applicable.

| No Treatment | Medication | Exercise | Meditation |
|---|---|---|---|
| 0 | 15 | 10 | 12 |
| 2 | 10 | 11 | 9 |
| 1 | 12 | 9 | 7 |
| 3 | 14 | 7 | 9 |
| 2 | 13 | 11 | 11 |
| 5 | 16 | 12 | 8 |
| 3 | 11 | 10 | 10 |
| 4 | 13 | 7 | 11 |
| 1 | 14 | 10 | 6 |
|  | 17 |  | 8 |

3. In problem 2, what is the purpose of having a group that receives no treatment?

## Post Test

1. In ANOVA, when the calculated $F$ ratio yields a value close to 1, what can be concluded?

2. If the null hypothesis is false, what is the nature of the relationship between variability between groups and variability within groups?

3. What is indicated by the relationship described in question 2?

4. How are differences between specific pairs of population means pinpointed?

5. When is it appropriate to use Scheffe's test?

6. Why is the $F$ test always nondirectional?

7. What are the assumptions that should be met in order to use the $F$ test?

8. What would be the result of violating the assumptions of the $F$ test?

9. In using Scheffe's test, what is the importance of sample size?

10. When would a researcher use the squared curvilinear correlation?

**Beyond the Basics**

Contemplate a research question that could best be answered by using ANOVA. What are some of the criteria you would want to meet? How many groups would be in your study? What treatment measures would you use? How would you select the participants? Would there be a control group? What variables might contribute to random error? What would sample size be? What should the level of significance be and when should it be established? Are there other questions you should ask yourself in preparing your study? Write a research proposal including the answers to these and any other pertinent questions that you develop.

# CHAPTER 23
# ANALYSIS OF VARIANCE (TWO WAY)

## Learning Objectives

- Develop knowledge and understanding of key terms.
- Calculate and interpret the $F$ test for two-way ANOVA.
- Determine appropriate situations when the two-way ANOVA should be used.

## Key Terms

**Two-way ANOVA**—A more complex type of analysis of variance that tests whether differences exist among population means categorized by two factors or independent variables.

**Main effect**—The effect of a single factor when any other factor is ignored.

**Simple effect**—The effect of one factor at a single level of another factor.

**Interaction**—The product of inconsistent simple effects.

## Text Review

In two-way ANOVA, there are four different types of means. Column means represent the effect of one variable when the other is ignored. In the text example, column means represent reaction times for each number of confederates present when (1)_____ is ignored. Slight differences among these column means could be attributed to (2)_____. More substantial differences reflect the main effect of the number of confederates on reaction time. In ANOVA, the effect of a single factor, when any other factor is ignored, is the (3)_____

_____. Row means represent the reaction times for gender when crowd size is ignored. Again, slight differences could be attributable to chance, but larger differences reflect a (4)_____ _____ of gender on reaction time. The cell means, also referred to as treatment-combination means, reflect any effect due to the interaction of the two factors being studied. The final average of the column means or row means equals the overall or (5)_____ _____.

You may recall from Chapter 22 that in one-way ANOVA, a single $F$ ratio is used to test the null hypothesis. In a two-way ANOVA, three different null hypotheses are tested, one at a time, with three $F$ ratios: $F_{column}$, $F_{row}$, $F_{interaction}$. In each $F$ ratio, the numerator represents (6)_____. This variability is random error or random error plus (7)_____ _____. The denominator term represents only (8)_____

_____ for subjects treated similarly in the same group.

With so many similarities between one-way and two-way ANOVA, (9)_____ is the most obvious different feature of two-way ANOVA. Two factors are said to interact if the effects of one factor are not consistent for all the levels of the second factor. The presence of interaction may highlight important issues for future research.

Interaction can be clarified by examining the concept of simple effect, the effect of one variable at a single level of another variable. Interaction is the product of (10)_____ simple effects.

The assumptions for the two-way ANOVA are similar to those for one-way ANOVA. All (11)_____ populations are assumed to be normally distributed with (12)_____ variances. You needn't be too concerned about violations of these assumptions as long as all group (13)_____ _____ are fairly large.

Although more complex ANOVA is possible with a larger number of factors, the goal of the researcher should be to use the simplest design that will adequately answer the research question.

The hypothesis test for two-way ANOVA has three null hypotheses, each of which can be retained or rejected. The decision rule must mention the decision criteria and critical value for rejecting each hypothesis, and each must be mentioned in the decision and interpretation. For a review, see the hypothesis test summary in your text.

The variance estimates in two-way ANOVA are similar to those in one-way ANOVA in that measures of variability always consist of a variance estimate or (14)_____ _____ calculated by dividing the sum of squares by its (15)_____ _____ _____. As in one-way ANOVA, the major computational effort is in calculating the various (16)_____ _____ _____ terms. For computational formulas for the various *SS* terms and *df* terms, see Table 23.2.

The same procedures used for one-way ANOVA also apply to two-way for obtaining critical *F* values from Table C, Appendix D.

Whenever interaction is present, as indicated by the (17)_____ of the null hypothesis for interaction, special statistical tests are usually conducted to pinpoint the precise location of the discrepancies that caused it. These special tests may be explored further in the Keppel book footnoted in your text. Differences between (18)_____ _____ and column means may also be examined with a modification of Scheffe's test for multiple comparisons.

## Problems and Exercises

1. An example problem presenting one-way ANOVA in Chapter 22 involved using $F$ to test the effect of the number of confederates present on sounding an alarm for smoke. Take this study further by adding the factor of whether the subjects grew up in rural or urban environments. Using the following data,

   a. Test the various null hypotheses at the .05 level of significance.
   b. Summarize the results with an ANOVA table.

| Environment | Number of Confederates | | |
|---|---|---|---|
| | **0** | **2** | **4** |
| **Rural** | 15 | 8 | 10 |
| | 13 | 11 | 3 |
| | 10 | 7 | 11 |
| | 16 | 9 | 12 |
| | 14 | 1 | 9 |
| **Urban** | | | |
| | 4 | 11 | 15 |
| | 8 | 16 | 18 |
| | 5 | 10 | 19 |
| | 7 | 11 | 17 |
| | 3 | 12 | 19 |

2. A military psychologist wishes to determine whether men are really better than women at spatial relations tasks, whether they are trained or untrained recruits. The four groups of six randomly assigned men and women are administered a ten-item spatial relations test. The data follow.

   a. Test the various null hypotheses at the .01 level of significance.

   b. Summarize the results with an ANOVA table.

| | Untrained Recruits | Trained Recruits |
|---|---|---|
| **Male** | 6 | 8 |
| | 6 | 6 |
| | 7 | 0 |
| | 4 | 5 |
| | 8 | 0 |
| | 8 | 9 |
| **Female** | 5 | 8 |
| | 5 | 6 |
| | 4 | 6 |
| | 3 | 6 |
| | 7 | 9 |
| | 3 | 5 |

## Post Test

1. In two-way ANOVA, if graphs are formed to reflect the possible effects, what is the meaning of slanted lines? What is the meaning of parallel lines?

2. In two-way ANOVA, what is represented by the numerator and denominator in the $F$ ratio?

3. What is the basis for rejecting the null hypothesis in two-way ANOVA?

4. What is the most striking feature of two-way ANOVA?

5. What are the assumptions for the $F$ tests in two-way ANOVA?

6. What happens if these assumptions are violated?

**Beyond the Basics**

Reread Section 23.11 in your text, describing interaction, paying close attention to the examples. Recall that interaction exists when the effects of one factor are not consistent for all levels of a second factor. Supply another example of factors that might interact from your own knowledge or experience. Try to determine how these factors could be set up for an experiment using ANOVA. Using the hypothesis test summary in your text as a model, write the research problem and statistical hypotheses. Set a level of significance and be prepared to defend your choice. Without any actual calculations (since you have no real data), predict an outcome and make a hypothetical decision to retain or reject the null hypotheses. Then write an interpretation based on your decision.

# CHAPTER 24
# CHI-SQUARE TEST FOR QUALITATIVE DATA

## Learning Objectives

- Develop knowledge and understanding of key terms.

- Determine appropriate situations for the use of chi-square for one- and two-variable cases.

- Calculate and interpret chi-square tests.

## Key Terms

**One-way test**—Evaluates whether observed frequencies for a single qualitative variable are adequately described by hypothesized or expected frequencies.

**Expected frequency**—The hypothesized frequency for each category, given that the null hypothesis is true.

**Observed frequency**—The obtained frequency for each category.

**Two-way test**—Evaluates whether observed frequencies reflect the independence of two qualitative variables.

**Squared Cramer's phi coefficient**—Very rough estimate of the proportion of predictability between two qualitative variables.

## Text Review

You may recall from Chapter 1, that when observations are classified into categories, the data are (1)_____. The hypothesis test for qualitative data is known as chi-square. When the variables are classified along a single variable, the test is a one-way chi-square. The one-

way chi-square test makes a statement about two or more population
(2)_____ that are reflected by expected frequencies.

If the null hypothesis is true, then except for the effects of chance, the hypothesized proportions should be reflected in the sample. The number of observations hypothesized is referred to as (3)_____ _____ and is calculated by multiplying the expected proportion by the total sample size. If the discrepancies between the observed and expected frequencies are small enough to be attributed to chance, then the null hypothesis would be retained. But if the discrepancies between the observed and expected frequencies are large enough to qualify as a rare outcome, the null hypothesis would be (4)_____.

The value of chi-square can never be (5)_____ because of the squaring of each difference between observed and expected frequencies.

For the one-way chi-square test, the degrees of freedom always equals the number of (6)_____ minus one.

The chi-square test is nondirectional because the squaring of the discrepancies always produces a (7)_____ value. However, for the same reason, only the upper tail of the sampling distribution contains the rejection region.

It is possible to cross-classify observations along two qualitative variables. This is referred to as a (8)_____ chi-square test. For the two-way test, the null hypothesis makes a statement about the lack of relationship between the two qualitative variables. In the two-way test, words

148

are usually used instead of symbols in the null hypothesis, and as in the one-way test, the research hypothesis simply states that the null hypothesis is false.

In the two-way test, expected frequencies are calculated by multiplying the column total times the row total and dividing by the overall total. The chi-square critical value may be found in Table D of Appendix D only if degrees of freedom are known. For the two-way test, degrees of freedom equals the number of categories for the column variable minus one, times the number of categories for the row variable minus one [$df = (C - 1)(R - 1)$].

Some precautions are necessary in using the chi-square tests. One restriction is that the chi-square test requires that observations be (9)_____. In this case, independence means that one observation should have no influence on another. One obvious violation of independence occurs when a single subject contributes more than one pair of observations. One way to check that this requirement is not being violated is to remember that the total for all observed frequencies must never exceed the total number of subjects. Using chi-square appropriately also requires that expected frequencies not be too small. Generally, any expected frequency of less than (10)_____ is too small. Small sample sizes should also be avoided, as should unduly large sample sizes. A sample size that is too large produces a test that detects differences of no practical importance.

When the null hypothesis has been rejected, the researcher should consider using squared (11)_____ phi coefficient to determine whether the strength of the relationship is small, medium, or large.

## Problems and Exercises

1. The American Automobile Association believes that the three long weekends with Monday holidays are equally dangerous in terms of traffic fatalities.

    a. Using the .05 level of significance, test the null hypothesis for the following data.

    b. Specify the $p$-value for the test result.

### Holiday Fatalities

| | Presidents' Day | Memorial Day | Labor Day |
|---|---|---|---|
| $f_o$ | 347 | 396 | 379 |

2. A researcher takes a sample of 200 students at a small college. The variable of ethnicity is significant to the research such that it must be determined whether or not the sample differs from the underlying population. School records indicate the following breakdown of the general student body: 60% white, 22% black, 13% Chicano, and 5% other.

   a. Using the following data from the research sample, test the null hypothesis at the .05 level of significance.
   b. Specify the $p$-value for the result.

### Ethnicity of College Students

| White | Black | Chicano | Other |
|-------|-------|---------|-------|
| 114   | 49    | 28      | 9     |

3. A sociologist examines the responses of 150 randomly selected people. The data are classified on the basis of religious preference (Catholic/Non-Catholic) and attitude toward abortion in extenuating circumstances (rape, risk to life or health of mother).

**Catholicism and Attitude Toward Abortion**

| Religion | Attitude Toward Abortion | | |
|---|---|---|---|
| | Favor | Oppose | Total |
| Non-Catholic | 52 | 23 | 75 |
| Catholic | 39 | 36 | 75 |
| Total | 91 | 59 | 150 |

    a. Using the .05 level of significance, test the null hypothesis that there is no relationship between religious preference and attitude toward abortion.

    b. Specify the $p$-value for the test result.

    c. Show how these results might appear in a published report.

4. A college professor wanted to investigate whether traditional students (age twenty-three and younger) preferred instructional methods that were different from those preferred by nontraditional students (age twenty-four and older).

    a. Test the following results using the .05 level of significance.
    b. Specify the $p$-value for the test result.
    c. Show how these results might appear in a published report.

### Instruction Methods

| Student | Lecture | Guest Speaker | Media | Group Study |
|---------|---------|---------------|-------|-------------|
| Traditional | 8 | 12 | 18 | 12 |
| Nontraditional | 17 | 11 | 14 | 8 |
| Total | 25 | 23 | 32 | 20 |

## Post Test

1. When the researcher wishes to determine whether a population complies with a single set of hypothesized proportions, which chi-square test should be used?

2. When the researcher wishes to test whether there is a relationship between two qualitative variables, which chi-square test should be used?

3. Why is the chi-square test nondirectional?

4. What are the conditions for use of the chi-square test?

5. What is the difference between expected frequency and observed frequency?

6. When would a researcher use squared Cramer's phi coefficient?

---

**Beyond the Basics**

The chi-square test represents a return to working with qualitative data. During the term, you may have thought of research questions dealing with qualitative data. If so, here is an opportunity to determine if chi-square would be an appropriate test to answer your question. If not, look back at the discussion of qualitative data in Chapter 1. Are there variables there representing qualitative data that are of interest to you? Discuss with one of your classmates or your instructor what areas of the behavioral sciences or other sciences might be most likely to use the chi-square test. Do some fields of study seem more likely than others? Which ones? Again, you might find more information by looking at professional journals in the library.

---

# CHAPTER 25
# TESTS FOR RANKED DATA

## Learning Objectives

- Develop knowledge and understanding of key terms.
- Determine appropriate situations for the use of tests for ranked data.
- Calculate and interpret the various tests for ranked data.

## Key Terms

**Mann-Whitney U test**—A test for ranked data when there are two independent groups.

**Wilcoxon T test**—A test for ranked data when there are two matched groups.

**Kruskal-Wallis H test**—A test for ranked data when there are more than two independent groups.

**Nonparametric tests**—Tests, such as $U$, $T$, and $H$, that evaluate entire population distributions rather than specific population characteristics.

**Distribution-free tests**—Tests, such as $U$, $T$, and $H$, that make no assumptions about the form of the population distribution.

## Text Review

In this chapter, the $U$, $T$, and $H$ tests are described. These tests are to be used with (1)_____ data. Furthermore, these tests can be used when underlying populations cannot be assumed to be normally distributed with equal variances.

The $U$, $T$, and $H$ tests, as well as the chi-square test, are referred to as nonparametric tests. (2) _____ refers to any descriptive measure of a population, such as a population mean. Nonparametric tests evaluate hypotheses for entire population distributions. The parametric tests like $t$ and $F$ evaluate hypotheses for a specific parameter, usually the population mean. Nonparametric tests may also be referred to as (3)_____ tests. The name signifies that these tests require no assumptions about the form of the population distribution. Remember, you have learned that $t$ and $F$ tests require that populations be normally distributed and have (4)_____ variances. The $U$, $T$, and $H$ tests make no such requirements.

When data are (5)_____ and the data are quantitative but don't seem to originate from normally distributed populations with equal variances, use $U$, $T$, and $H$ tests. When the data are (6)_____ and the populations appear to be normally distributed with equal variances, use $t$ and $F$ tests. Under the appropriate assumptions, $t$ and $F$ are more likely to detect a false null hypothesis, thus minimizing the chance of a (7)_____ ____ _____ error.

The Mann-Whitney $U$ test is used when there are two independent samples. The familiar $t$ test cannot be used because the assumptions of (8)_____ and equal variances have been violated. This would affect the probability of a (9)_____ ____ _____.
The data are converted to ranks to avoid this problem. Using the ranks, the null hypothesis equates the two entire population (10)_____. Therefore, any type of inequality between the population distributions could cause the rejection of the null

156

hypothesis. If it can be assumed that the two population distributions have about equal variability and similar shapes, then rejecting the null hypothesis would indicate that the difference between the two is likely to be difference in central tendency or difference in population (11)_____.

When all estimates in the two groups have been assigned ranks, the groups can be compared to form a preliminary impression. The more one group outranks the other, the larger the difference between the mean ranks for the two groups, the more likely the null hypothesis will be (12)_____. The calculated value for $U$ is compared with the critical value found in Table E of Appendix D. The decision rule is unusual in that the null hypothesis will be rejected only if the observed $U$ is (13)_____ than or equal to the critical $U$. This is the opposite of the decision rule for all other tests presented so far in this text.

The $U$ test can be either directional or nondirectional. However, when a directional test is desired, the researcher must meet the assumption of similar (14)_____ and (15)_____. One caution that should be observed when using the directional test is that the researcher must make sure that differences in the population distributions are in the direction of concern.

If there are (16)_____ variables that could affect the outcome of the study, the subjects could be matched. The matching creates two matched samples that require the Wilcoxon $T$ test. The familiar $t$ test cannot be used because the data in the text example are skewed, thus violating the assumption of (17)_____ required for $t$. The null hypothesis for $T$ is like that for $U$ in that it equates the two (18)_____ _____. The rejection of the null hypothesis indicates only that the two populations differ. Again, if similar variability and shapes can be assumed, more precise conclusions are possible.

The observed value for $T$ is compared to the critical $T$ found in Table F of Appendix D. The $T$ test may be either directional or (19)_____. As with $U$, the null hypothesis will be rejected only if the observed $T$ is (20)_____ than or equal to the critical $T$.

When there are three or more independent groups, the Kruskal-Wallis $H$ test must be used if the assumptions of (21)_____ and equal (22)_____ cannot be assured. In this test, unless sample sizes are very small, the critical values of $H$ are obtained from the chi-square distribution (Table D, Appendix D). This requires degrees of freedom for $H$, $df$ = number of groups – 1. Unlike $U$ and $T$, the decision rule for $H$ returns to the more familiar pattern. The null hypothesis will be rejected if the observed $H$ is equal to or greater than the critical chi-square. Because the sums of the ranks are squared, the $H$ test is always (23)_____.

# Problems and Exercises

1. Can parental training in behavior modification techniques improve first graders' classroom behavior? Sixteen first graders were randomly assigned to two groups, one whose parents received behavior modification training and one whose parents did not. Two months after the training, the first-grade teacher was asked to rank the sixteen children on compliance to teacher requests.

## Compliance Ranking of First Graders

| Trained Parents | Untrained Parents |
|:---:|:---:|
| 1 | 11 |
| 3.5 | 14.5 |
| 9 | 16 |
| 3 | 10 |
| 3.5 | 14.5 |
| 7 | 6 |
| 2 | 8 |
| 5 | 12 |

   a. Use $U$ to test the null hypothesis at the .05 level of significance.
   b. Specify the $p$-value for the test result.
   c. Interpret your results.

2. A team of psychologists worked with students on the problem of test anxiety. Using the Swinn Test Anxiety Behavior Scale, test anxiety was measured before and after a series of group workshops and individual therapy to reduce anxiety. The following results were obtained:

**Swinn Test Anxiety Behavior Scale Scores**

| Student | Before | After |
|---------|--------|-------|
| 1 | 120 | 105 |
| 2 | 135 | 100 |
| 3 | 145 | 115 |
| 4 | 160 | 125 |
| 5 | 120 | 110 |
| 6 | 150 | 120 |
| 7 | 135 | 110 |

a. Use $T$ to test the null hypothesis at the .05 level of significance.
b. Specify the $p$-value for the test result.
c. Interpret your results.

3. A consumers' group continues its interest in motion picture ratings. After the films were screened for violence and sexually explicit scenes, an additional screening was done by the trained observer to count the number of expletives in each film. The following results were obtained.

**Number of Expletives in Films**

| X | R | PG-13 | PG | G |
|---|---|-------|----|----|
| 12 | 17 | 15 | 10 | 2 |
| 8 | 22 | 13 | 7 | 0 |
| 7 | 19 | 11 | 5 | 3 |
| 10 | 19 | 17 | 8 | 3 |
| 7 | 21 | 15 | 7 | 1 |

a. Use $H$ to test the null hypothesis at the .05 level of significance.
b. Specify the $p$-value for the test result.
c. Interpret your results.

4. The principal of an elementary school wishes to determine the most effective method to improve reading as measured by the district's reading achievement test. Twenty-eight children in third grade are randomly assigned to one of three reading improvement programs. Test the difference between their September reading scores and April reading scores to determine whether any one method is superior. Use the .05 level of significance. The difference scores follow. You may recognize this problem from Chapter 19.

    a. Instead of the $F$ test, just for practice, test the null hypothesis using the $H$ test.
    b. Specify the $p$-value for the test result.
    c. Interpret your results.

| Tutoring | Home Help | Reading Aloud |
|:---:|:---:|:---:|
| 10 | 8 | 6 |
| 7 | 6 | 9 |
| 12 | 4 | 5 |
| 9 | 4 | 7 |
| 13 | 9 | 7 |
| 11 | 7 | 6 |
| 10 | 8 | 8 |
| 14 | 5 | 5 |
| 11 | 7 | 9 |
|  | 8 |  |

# Post Test

1. What test is used for ranked data with two independent samples?

2. What test is appropriate for ranked data using two matched samples?

3. Why are these tests used instead of $t$?

4. What is distinctive about the decision rules for both the Mann Whitney $U$ and the Wilcoxon $T$ tests?

5. What is a nonparametric test?

6. What is a distribution-free test?

7. Which of the tests studied in this chapter seems to replace ANOVA under specific circumstances?

## Beyond the Basics

To help you really understand the nonparametric tests, make a chart comparing each of the nonparametric tests with its parametric counterpart. For example, compare $t$ with $U$. You would want to include information such as the assumptions for each test, the type of data appropriate for use with the test, how to determine critical values, and how to make the decision to retain or reject $H_0$.

# CHAPTER 26
# POSTSCRIPT: WHICH TEST?

## Learning Objectives

Determine which statistical analysis is appropriate to answer a particular research question.

## Text Review

If you are attempting a research project of your own, you will probably be selecting a statistical test from among the ones you have studied so far. The following is a review of some important ideas and a look at some questions you might ask in order to select the appropriate test.

What is the intent of your study? If you wish to summarize existing data, you will be using (1)_____ statistics. If you wish to generalize beyond existing data, you will be using (2)_____ statistics.

In the behavioral sciences, hypothesis tests are usually preferred to confidence intervals. However, even if you follow this preference, if the null hypothesis is rejected, consider estimating the possible size of the effect by constructing a (3)_____ _____.

When deciding which test to use, it must be determined whether the observations are quantitative or qualitative. If the data are (4)_____, the appropriate hypothesis test should be selected from the various $t$ or $F$ tests or their nonparametric counterparts.

When the observations are (5)_____, the appropriate test will be the chi-square.

Sometimes the decision as to whether the data are qualitative or quantitative is not so easy. If you are not sure, use the following guidelines to help make your decision. (1) Focus on a single observation. (2) Focus on numerical summaries. (3) Focus on key words.

Once the nature of the data has been decided, another question to be resolved in selecting the appropriate test is the number of groups. If only one group is involved, then a (6)_____ test for a single population is appropriate. If there are two groups, a $t$ test may also be appropriate, but you must decide whether the groups are matched or independent. If the concern of the researcher is to determine whether paired observations are significantly correlated, then the appropriate test is the $t$ test for a population correlation coefficient. When there are more than two groups, the $F$ test for (7)_____ is the correct choice. The ANOVA test can be either one-way or (8)_____-_____.

Finally, the nonparametric tests are to be used when the original observations are (9)_____ or when some assumption is violated.

## Problems and Exercises

Here are some additional exercises to provide practice in identifying the appropriate statistical test. As with the exercises in the text, no assumptions have been violated unless noted otherwise. For each example, be sure to specify all you know about the type of test. For instance, specify that the $t$ test is for a single population mean, or that chi-square is one-way or two-way.

1. A researcher wishes to determine the relationship between scores on the GED test and scores on the ACT.

2. An investigator wishes to determine whether drinking alcohol impairs memory. Before a test of short-term memory, subjects drank a glass of juice. For one group, the juice was straight, and for the other group, the juice contained two ounces of vodka. The volunteer subjects were randomly assigned to the two groups. The mean performance was computed for each group.

3. The preceding experiment was repeated using the same subjects for both conditions. On Monday half the subjects drank the plain juice and performed a short-term memory test, and the other half drank the juice with the alcohol and then performed the memory test. On the following day, the procedure was repeated according to counterbalancing requirements. The mean performances were computed.

4. Do male and female college students desire different characteristics in a spouse? The students are surveyed as to what characteristics they most desire. Responses of male and female students indicate that sense of humor, looks, loyalty, wealth, and educational level are important to both sexes, but not necessarily in equal proportion.

5. A developmental psychologist wishes to examine the relationship between age and reaction time. Three groups of subjects are tested on a measure of reaction time and their performances are compared. Subjects in group 1 are ten years old. Group 2 subjects are forty years old, and group 3 subjects are seventy years old.

6. A psychobiologist wishes to test the visual performance of mice after varying periods of light deprivation. At birth, the mice are randomly assigned to periods of zero, one, two, or three months of light deprivation. Trained observer rates the mice' performance in a visually challenging maze. A mean performance is computed for each group.

7. A psychology professor wishes to determine whether the test performance of statistics students is affected by special tutoring after class. The students are randomly assigned either to a tutoring group or to a group that meets after class socially but does not study or discuss course material. The test performances of group members are ranked.

8. The statistics students are randomly assigned to a test anxiety workshop in a group or to individual therapy to reduce the test anxiety. The researcher wishes to determine which method best reduces the test anxiety scores.

9. A researcher wishes to determine the relationship between scores on a love scale and number of years of marriage.


10. A director of institutional research wishes to determine whether students' math exam grades are higher when math classes are taught twice a week for one and a half hours, once a week for three hours, or three times a week for fifty minutes.

# ANSWERS

## Chapter 1

### Text Review

1. descriptive
2. inferential
3. data
4. quantitative
5. qualitative
6. qualitative
7. independent
8. dependent
9. cause-effect
10. correlations

### Problems and Exercises

#### I. Qualitative or Quantitative Data

1. qualitative
2. quantitative
3. quantitative
4. qualitative
5. qualitative
6. quantitative
7. qualitative
8. qualitative
9. quantitative
10. quantitative

#### II. Descriptive or Inferential Statistics

| | | | | |
|---|---|---|---|---|
| 1. D | 2. D | 3. I | 4. D | 5. I |
| 6. D | 7. I | 8. D | 9. I | 10. D |

#### III. Correlation or Experiment

1. correlation
2. experiment
   dependent variable : test anxiety
   independent variable : hypnosis
3. experiment
   dependent variable : reaction time
   independent variable : amount of alcohol

## Post Test

1. descriptive, inferential
2. descriptive
3. inferential
4. data
5. quantitative
6. qualitative
7. independent
8. experiment
9. dependent
10. correlation

# Chapter 2

## Text Review

1. single
2. smallest
3. largest
4. grouped
5. one
6. equal
7. boundaries
8. convenient
9. ten
10. unit of measurement
11. relative
12. cumulative frequency
13. percentile rank
14. approximate
15. descending
16. relative frequency
17. outliers
18. footnotes

## Problems and Exercises

1.

## Table 2.1

| grades | f | relative f | cumulative f | cumulative % |
|--------|---|-----------|--------------|--------------|
| 48-50 | 2 | .07 | 30 | 100 |
| 45-47 | 2 | .07 | 28 | 93 |
| 42-44 | 4 | .13 | 26 | 87 |
| 39-41 | 7 | .23 | 22 | 73 |
| 36-38 | 4 | .13 | 15 | 50 |
| 33-35 | 4 | .13 | 11 | 37 |
| 30-32 | 4 | .13 | 7 | 23 |
| 27-29 | 2 | .07 | 3 | 10 |
| 24-26 | 0 | .00 | 1 | 3 |
| 21-23 | 1 | .03 | 1 | 3 |

2. The interval of 36-38
3. Grouped, there are more than twenty possible values.
4. In general, the most frequencies occurred in the interval of 39-41. This would be a percentage correct of about 78 to 82 on the test. However, over one third, eleven people, scored below 35, which would be 70 percent correct. If 70 percent is passing, perhaps the professor would not be pleased that only 19 out of 30 students passed the test. She might also like to see more high grades in the intervals of 45-47 and 48-50.
5. The unit of measurement is one score point.
6. The score at the 73rd percentile means that of all the people who took the test, this boy scored higher than or equal to 73 percent of them. He is better in reading than in math when compared to his peers.

## Post Test

1. frequency distribution for ungrouped data
2. twenty
3. information about each observation is lost
4. the distribution fails to provide a concise description of the data
5. the unit of measurement
6. relative frequency
7. percentile rank
8. ranked or ordered
9. outlier

# Chapter 3

## Text Review

1. frequency distributions
2. histogram
3. equal
4. class intervals
5. increases in frequency
6. zero
7. increase
8. frequency polygon
9. distributions
10. stem and leaf display
11. frequency table
12. histogram
13. raw scores
14. shape
15. bell
16. bimodal
17. positively
18. negatively
19. minority
20. bar graph
21. different words/classes
22. frequency
23. gaps
24. about equal
25. about equal
26. zero

# Problems and Exercises

1.

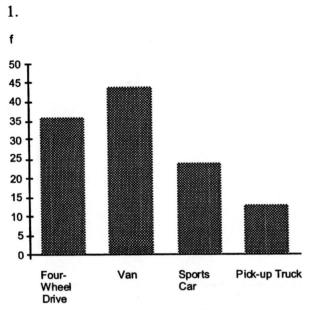

Comfort of Housewives in Different Vehicles

2.

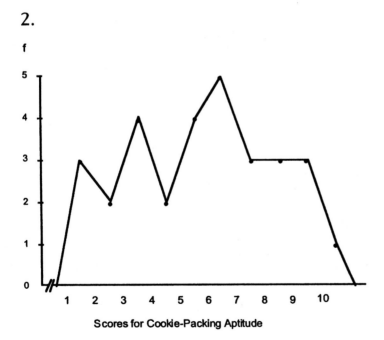

Scores for Cookie-Packing Aptitude

3.

a.

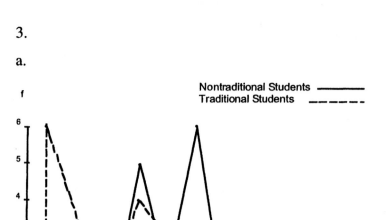

f

Nontraditional Students ⎯⎯⎯⎯⎯
Traditional Students ⎯ ⎯ ⎯ ⎯ ⎯

66–68  69–71  72–74  75–77  78–80  81–83  84–86  87–89  90–92  93–95  96–98

Test Results of Traditional versus Nontraditional

b. The distribution for nontraditional students is somewhat positively skewed.
c. The distribution for traditional students is the same.
d. Overall, the performance of the two groups is very similar.

## Post Test

1. A bar graph is used when the data are qualitative and a histogram when the data are quantitative.
2. Three ways to make misleading graphs:
   a. radically unequal axes
   b. omit the lower end of the frequency scale
   c. unequal size of the bars on the graph
3. Skewness is always in the direction of the minority of observations.
4. Frequency polygons are particularly useful when comparing two or more distributions.
5. The gaps in the bar graph illustrate the discontinuous nature of the qualitative data.
6. The stem and leaf display has the advantage of maintaining the information represented by the raw scores.

# Chapter 4

## Text Review

| | |
|---|---|
| 1. measures of central tendency | 2. mode |
| 3. prevalent or fashionable | 4. bimodal |
| 5. multimodal | 6. differences or subsets |
| 7. median | 8. 50 |
| 9. value | 10. mean |
| 11. mean | 12. $\bar{X}$(mean) |
| 13. •(sum of) | 14. $X$ |
| 15. 0 | 16. population |
| 17. sample | 18. not too skewed |
| 19. tendency | 20. central tendency |
| 21. mode | 22. median |
| 23. mean | 24. skewed |
| 25. positively | 26. negatively |
| 27. mean | 28. mode |
| 29. median | 30. mean |

## Problems and Exercises

1. Only the mode is appropriate, as this is qualitative data that cannot be ranked.
2. mean = 33.67     mode = 23     median = 33
3. mean = 5.87      mode = 6      median = 6
4. mean = 87.36     mode = 93     median = 89.5
5. mean = 35.30     mode = 20     median = 29

## Post Test

1. mean and median
2. mode always, median if the data can be ranked
3. the mode
4. $\bar{X}$
5.

6. a bimodal distribution indicates differences or subsets among the observations in the distribution
7. both the mean and the median
8. mean
9. negatively

# Chapter 5

## Text Review

1. range
2. calculated
3. only two observations
4. increase
5. standard deviation
6. variability
7. mean
8. definition
9. computation
10. square root
11. variance
12. original
13. rough
14. average
15. mean
16. 68
17. 5
18. position
19. distance
20. negative
21. interquartile range
22. 50 percent
23. extreme observations
24. outliers
25. nonexistent

## Problems and Exercises

1. $S = 10.00$, $S^2 = 100.06$
2. a. 24 and 44      b. 14 and 54      c. 44
   d. within one standard deviation in the positive direction (above the mean)
   e. within two standard deviations in the negative direction
3. the range = 33
4. the range = 26      standard deviation = 7.71
5. the range = 35      standard deviation = 10.5

## Post Test

1. Two limitations of the range are (a) it increases as the number of observations increases and (b) it is based on only two observations.
2. The standard deviation is the preferred measure of variability because of the previously discussed limitations of the range and the fact that the variance distorts the unit of measure and the standard deviation does not.

3. Measures of variability for qualitative data are virtually nonexistent.
4. When the mean is a complex value or the data set contains a large number of observations, the computation formula is preferred.
5. The advantage of the interquartile range is that it is not sensitive to extreme values.

# Chapter 6

## Text Review

1. theoretical
2. symmetrical
3. mirror
4. midway
5. infinitely
6. normally distributed
7. mean
8. standard deviation
9. $z$ scores
10. mean
11. mean
12. standard deviation
13. zero
14. one
15. proportions
16. .5000
17. 1.000

## Problems and Exercises

1. a. 2.33    b. .50    c. -.67    d. 1.17    e. -.33
2. a. .0918    b. .7794    c. .1915    d. .4990

## Post Test

1. symmetrical, bell-shaped
2. mean/standard deviation
3. $z$ score
4. standard normal curve
5. column B
6. .5000
6. 1.000

# Chapter 7

## Text Review

1. proportion
2. scores
3. logic
4. normal curve
5. sketch
6. solution
7. $z$ scores
8. smaller
9. scores
10. mean
11. positive
12. negative
13. common
14. rare

## Problems and Exercises

1. $z = -1.67$, under C' column area = .0475 = 5%
2. $z = .66$, under B column area = .2454, add to .5000 for lower half of curve = .7454 = 75%
3. When C = .07, $z = 1.48$ because .0694 is closer to .07 than .0708 is, $\bar{X}$= 26.88 or 27. Note: It is important to round off to 27, as ACT scores are reported in whole numbers. Keep in mind the original unit of measure when reporting values of $X$.
4. .0228
5. .4332
6. 17.26 pounds

## Post Test

1. It helps to visualize the solution.
2. finding proportions and finding scores
3. increases
4. above

# Chapter 8

## Text Review

1. standard normal table
2. zero
3. one
4. reference
5. standard
6. decimals
7. negative signs
8. 50
9. 10
10. IQ
11. GRE
12. 50
13. standard scores

## Problems and Exercises

1. a. 73.30     b. 55     c. 43.30     d. 61.70     e. 46.70
2. a. 6915 or 69%          b. .8849 or 88%          c. .0968 or 10%
3. a. 115     b. 100          c. 94
4. Mary's $z$ score is 1.67, higher than Bob's score of 1.5 and Jim's score of 1.4.

## Post Test

1. $z$ scores may be appropriately used with non-normal distributions, but the standard normal table can only be used with normal distributions.
2. zero/one
3. the nature of the reference group
4. they lack decimals and negative signs
5. the scale of percentile ranks does not increase in equal increments

# Chapter 9

## Text Review

1. positive
2. negative
3. scatterplot
4. positive
5. negative
6. no relationship
7. stronger
8. linear
9. curvilinear
10. $r$
11. -1
12. +1
13. positive
14. negative
15. strength
16. Pearson $r$
17. positive
18. negative
19. value
20. laboratory experiment
21. Spearman's rho
22. point biserial
23. Cramer's phi
24. correlation matrix

## Problems and Exercises

1. a. $r = -.90$
   b. Effects of chance, practice, motivation, fatigue, and other factors are also possible.
2. The scatterplot is approximately linear, sloping from upper left to lower right.
3. a. Reasonably strong positive
   b. There appears to be a strong positive relationship between study time and performance on statistics exams.
   c. Test anxiety, health, fatigue, motivation, and other worries or stress, to name a few
4. b. $r = .398$, or .40        c. The scatterplot is an inverted U.

## Post Test

1. -1 to +1
2. No relationship between the two variables
3. Correlation can never show cause and effect
4. Perfect positive relationship
5. correlation matrix
6. curvilinear

# Chapter 10

## Text Review

1. unknown
2. prediction
3. least squares regression
4. least squares prediction
5. $Y' = bX + a$
6. predicted
7. known
8. descriptive
9. least squares prediction equation
10. standard error of prediction
11. zero
12. strong
13. low
14. assumptions
15. linear
16. curvilinear
17. homoscedasticity
18. normally
19. correlation coefficient
20. strength

## Problems and Exercises

1. a. $Y' = (b)(X) + a = (.90)(X) + -.13$
   b. 1.19
   c. $Y' = (.90)(11) + -.13 = 9.77$, or 10 ringers
   d. $Y' = (.90)(5) + (-.13)$
      $Y' = 4.50 -.13 = 4.37$, or 4 ringers

## Post Test

| 1. true | 2. false | 3. true | 4. true | 5. true |
|---------|----------|---------|---------|---------|
| 6. true | 7. true | 8. false | 9. true | 10. false |

# Chapter 11

## Text Review

1. real
2. hypothetical
3. accessible
4. not accessible
5. sampling
6. sample
7. variability
8. error
9. random
10. observations
11. equal
12. representative
13. fishbowl
14. stirred
15. random
16. population size
17. large
18. random
19. uncontrolled variables
20. equal
21. pairs

## Problems and Exercises

1. a. Yes.
   b. The bouncing of the balls is the equivalent of stirring in the "fishbowl" method. It helps to insure that each ball has an equal chance of being the next one selected.
   c. The clear container assures participants that all fifty balls are there and that they are marked appropriately, etc.
2. a. Assign them in pairs. If the first subject is assigned to the control group, then the second automatically goes to the experimental group.
   b. Numbers 1, 2, and 3 could be assigned to the control group, and numbers 4, 5, and 6 could be assigned to the experimental group.

## Post Test

1. All observations are represented on slips of paper. The slips are placed in a container and stirred thoroughly. Slips are drawn one at a time until the desired sample size is reached.
2. A sample is random if all the observations in the population have an equal chance of being selected.
3. Random assignment is done to ensure that groups of subjects are similar with respect to any uncontrolled variables.

4. A real population is one in which all observations are accessible at the time of sampling. A hypothetical population is one in which all observations are not accessible.
5. You must determine where to enter the table, which direction to read, and how many digits to use.

# Chapter 12

## Text Review

| | |
|---|---|
| 1. probability | 2. speculation |
| 3. observation | 4. zero |
| 5. one | 6. one |
| 7. addition | 8. multiplication |
| 9. mutually exclusive | 10. multiplication |
| 11. independent | 12. conditional |
| 13. probabilities | 14. statistical significance |
| 15. rare | |

## Problems and Exercises

1. a. .50     b. 1.00     c. addition     d. 1/6, or .17     e. 2/6 or .33
2. a. .25 x .25 x .25 x .25 = .0039
   b. .75 x .75 x .75 x .75 = .3164
   c. Use questions with five answer choices.
3. Because the probability of a correct guess on a true-false question is .50, but on a four-option multiple-choice question, the probability of a correct guess is .25.
4. Three. No matter what color is selected first or second, the third one will match one of the other two. This is a logic problem that requires no calculation. However, it should give you practice in seeing what's important and what's not. In this case, the ratio of 4 to 5 has nothing to do with solving the problem.

## Post Test

1. Probabilities can range in value from 0 to 1.
2. All probabilities in a set sum to 1.
3. With mutually exclusive outcomes, use the addition rule.
4. The multiplication rule should be used with independent outcomes.
5. Since probabilities represent the area under the curve, we can use the standard normal table ($z$ table) to determine exact positions along the horizontal base line corresponding to the area or probability. We can then determine the probability that a particular value will fall within the range

of specific $z$ scores. For instance, the standard normal table indicates that .95 is the proportion of the area under the curve that falls between $z$ scores of -1.96 and +1.96.

# Chapter 13

## Text Review

| | |
|---|---|
| 1. common | 2. rare |
| 3. mean | 4. standard deviation |
| 5. mean | 6. standard deviation |
| 7. standard error of the mean | 8. population |
| 9. standard error of the mean | 10. standard deviation |
| 11. sample size | 12. variability |
| 13. larger | 14. 25/100 |

## Problems and Exercises

| | | | | |
|---|---|---|---|---|
| 1. true | 2. false | 3. false | 4. true | 5. true |
| 6. false | 7. true | 8. true | 9. true | 10. false |
| 11. true | 12. true | | | |

## Post Test

1. a. mean of the sampling distribution      $\mu_{\bar{x}}$
   b. population mean      $\mu$
   c. standard error of the mean      $\sigma_{\bar{x}}$
   d. sample mean      $\bar{X}$
   e. population standard deviation      $\sigma$

2. As sample size increases, variability decreases.
3. Standard error of the mean is a rough measure of the average amount by which sample means deviate from the mean of the sampling distribution (or the population mean).
4. 25 to 100
5. They are always equal in value.

# Chapter 14

## Text Review

1. common
2. retained
3. rare
4. $z$ score
5. standard normal distribution
6. central limit
7. research problem
8. null
9. population
10. null
11. research
12. decision rule
13. level of significance
14. interpreted

## Problems and Exercises

1. $H_0: \mu = 76$
   $H_1: \mu \neq 76$
   Reject $H_0$ at the .05 level of significance if $z$ equals or is more positive than 1.96 or if $z$ equals or is more negative than -1.96.
   $z = 3.39$
   Reject $H_0$.
   Interpretation: The average age of Texas nursing home residents differs from the national average.

2. $H_0: \mu \bullet 100$
   $H_1: \mu > 100$
   Reject $H_0$ at the .05 level of significance if $z$ equals or is more positive than 1.65.
   $z = 3.07$
   Reject $H_0$.
   Interpretation: The average IQ of students in the local school district exceeds the national average.

3. $H_0: \mu = 18$
   $H_1: \mu \neq 18$
   Reject $H_0$ at the .05 level of significance if $z$ equals or is more positive than 1.96 or if $z$ equals or is more negative than -1.96.
   $z = 2.60$

Reject $H_0$.

Interpretation: The average ACT score of students at the B.A. Nurse RN school differs from the national average.

## Post Test

1. Converting to $z$ eliminates the original units of measure and standardizes the hypothesis testing procedure across all situations.
2. a. The population must be normally distributed or sample size must be large enough to meet the central limit theorem.
   b. The population standard deviation must be known.
3. null
4. alternative
5. decision rule
6. level of significance
7. State the research problem.
   Identify the statistical hypothesis.
   Specify a decision rule.
   Calculate the value of the observed $z$.
   Make a decision.
   Interpret the decision.

# Chapter 15

## Text Review

1. generalize
2. standard error
3. type I error
4. type II
5. strong
6. nondirectional
7. two-tailed
8. one-tailed

## Problems and Exercises

1. standard error
2. The decision to retain the null hypothesis is considered weak because the hypothesized value could be true and so could other similar values.
3. The research hypothesis lacks the necessary precision to be tested directly. The research hypothesis is identified with the alternative hypothesis and, therefore, the decision to reject the null hypothesis will provide strong support for the research hypothesis.
4. The .05 level of significance is customary, but a level of .01 or .001 can be used when a type I error would have serious consequences.
5. The researcher chooses a one-tailed test when certain that there is a concern only about deviations in one particular direction.

## Post Test

| | | | | |
|---|---|---|---|---|
| 1. true | 2. true | 3. false | 4. true | 5. true |
| 6. false | 7. false | 8. true | 9. true | 10. false |

# Chapter 16

## Text Review

1. correct decision
2. true
3. type I error
4. type II error
5. effect
6. true
7. type I
8. alpha
9. 1–alpha
10. false alarms
11. miss
12. beta
13. large
14. 1–beta
15. small
16. sample size
17. standard error
18. effect
19. power curves

## Problems and Exercises

1. After the researcher has decided to retain $H_o$, he has either made a correct decision or a type II error. If the researcher decides to reject $H_o$, he has either made a correct decision or a type I error.
2. The researcher should reduce sample size or decrease alpha to .01, or both. As it is, the experiment may produce results that are statistically significant but of no practical importance.
3. 1-alpha
4. 1-beta
5. Increase sample size.
6. The size of the effect. The smaller the effect, the greater the probability of a type II error and the smaller the probability of a correct decision.
7. The researcher can alter sample size or determine alpha level, which affects the probability of correct decisions or errors. But the size of the effect relies simply on the outcome of the experiment and cannot be manipulated.

## Post Test

| | | | | |
|---|---|---|---|---|
| 1. true | 2. true | 3. false | 4. true | 5. false |
| 6. false | 7. true | 8. true | | |

# Chapter 17

## Text Review

1. point estimates
2. confidence intervals
3. population
4. inaccurate
5. sampling variability
6. confidence intervals
7. population mean
8. population mean
9. sample size
10. central limit theorem
11. population standard deviation
12. 25
13. true
14. false
15. precise
16. sample size
17. 95
18. 99
19. confidence intervals
20. effect
21. effect
22. margin of error
23. experiment

## Problems and Exercises

1. $\bar{X} + (z_{conf})\,(\sigma_{\bar{x}}) =$
   $79 + (1.96)\,(.5) =$
   $79 + .98 = 78.02$ to $79.98$
   $\sigma_{\bar{x}} = .5$
   We can claim with 95 percent confidence that the interval between 78.02 and 79.98 includes the true population mean age.
2. a. 108
   b. $\bar{X} + (z_{conf})\,(\sigma_{\bar{x}}) ==$
      $108 + (2.58)\,(2.61) =$
      $108 + 6.73 = 101.27$ to $114.73$
      $\sigma_{\bar{x}} = 2.61$
   c. We can claim with 99 percent confidence that the interval between 101.27 and 114.73 includes the true population mean IQ.
3. a. The confidence interval is too wide.
   b. To make the confidence interval more precise, switch to a lesser degree of confidence such as 90 percent or increase the sample size.

## Post Test

1. Both hypothesis tests and confidence intervals are more precise with larger samples. Both rely on values of $z$ from the standard normal table. Both are based on properties of the sampling distribution listed for answer 3.

2. In experiments, the larger sample makes the hypothesis test more sensitive, so that the null hypothesis will almost always be rejected. This leads to the detection of an effect that may have statistical significance but no practical importance. Furthermore, experimentation may involve some very expensive and time-consuming procedures that would have to be applied to all members of the sample. In polls and surveys, the viewpoint is that the larger the sample is the better since increases are more likely to create samples that accurately reflect the characteristic of the population. Also, in polls and surveys, the information-gathering techniques provide easy and inexpensive answers to questions, thus foregoing the problems of time and expense faced by experimenters.

3. Three important properties of confidence intervals must be understood. (1) The mean of the sampling distribution always equals the population mean. (2) The standard error of the sampling distribution equals the population standard deviation divided by the square root of the sample size. (3) The shape of the sampling distribution approximates a normal distribution if sample size satisfies the central limit theorem.

4. The use of formula 17.1 assumes that the population standard deviation is known and that the population is normal or that sample size is sufficiently large to meet the requirements of the central limit theorem.

5. As sample size increases, standard error decreases, and the confidence interval becomes more precise.

6. A point estimate specifies a single value for the unknown population mean, whereas the confidence interval supplies a range of values.

7. Point estimates are inaccurate because they do not take into account sampling variability.

# Chapter 18

## Text Review

1. William Gossett
2. degrees of freedom
3. sample size minus one
4. inflated tails
5. positive
6. upper
7. larger
8. rejected
9. retained
10. population standard deviation
11. normally distributed
12. sample size
13. descriptive
14. inferential
15. n–1
16. degrees of freedom
17. zero

## Problems and Exercises

1.  a. using a one-tailed test, upper tail critical, $t = 1.95$; reject the null hypothesis.
    b. The 95 percent confidence interval = 67.86 – 89.0
    c. It can be claimed with 95 percent confidence that the interval between 67.86 and 89.0 includes the true mean grade for summer students.
2.  a. ±3.646  b. 2.518  c. 1.860
3.  a. 3.3    b. 2.33   c. 1.65
    $z$ values are smaller than $t$ values because of the inflated tails of the $t$ distribution.
4.  a. using a one-tailed test, upper tail critical $t = 2.22$; reject the null hypothesis.
    b. The 95 percent confidence interval equals 20.6 – 29.4.
    c. It can be claimed with 95 percent confidence that the interval between 20.6 and 29.4 includes the true mean number of pockets sewed.
    d. Yes, because production is increased when the fixed ratio reinforcement schedule is used.

## Post Test

1. A *t* test should be used when the population standard deviation is unknown.
2. The inflated tails of the *t* distribution cause *t* values to be larger than *z* values, especially if sample size is small.
3. To use *t*, you must assume that the underlying population is normally distributed.
4. If the assumption of normality is violated, the *t* test will retain most of its accuracy as long as sample size is sufficiently large (larger than ten).
5 Degrees of freedom refers to the number of values, within a set of values, which are free to vary, given some mathematical restriction. Specifically, in a *t* test, degrees of freedom are related to the estimate of the population standard deviation and the use of $n - 1$ in the denominator of the formula for that estimate.

# Chapter 19

## Text Review

1. observations
2. effect
3. blood doping
4. no
5. nondirectional
6. lower
7. upper
8. exceeds
9. directional
10. hypothesis test
11. population
12. difference
13. standard error
14. population means
15. increases
16. equal
17. no effect
18. normally distributed
19. equal
20. fairly large/equal
21. observations
22. deviations

## Problems and Exercises

1. Using a nondirectional or two-tailed test $t = -3.45$; reject the null hypothesis.
2. Using a nondirectional or two-tailed test $t = 6.17$; reject the null hypothesis.

## Post Test

1. a. The mean of the sampling distribution equals the difference between population means.
   b. The standard error roughly measures the average amount by which any difference between sample means deviates from the difference between population means.
2. Degrees of freedom is $n_1 + n_2 - 2$.
3. When the two limits of the interval share similar signs. Both are either positive or negative.
4. Both underlying populations are normally distributed with equal variances.

# Chapter 20

## Text Review

1. paired
2. One/sample
3. difference scores
4. zero
5. exceeds
6. less
7. difference scores
8. variability
9. variability
10. standard error
11. increases
12. pilot studies
13. repeated measures
14. counterbalancing
15. sample size
16. bivariate

## Problems and Exercises

1. $t = 4.10$; rejecthe null hypothesis
2. Using a two tailedtest, a. $t = -8.035$; reject the null hypothesis
   b. $p < .001$
3. Using a one-tailed test, upper tail critical, $t = 3.856$; reject the null hypothesis, $p < .01$
   c. The samples are dependent because we could think of identical twins as being matched on all hereditary characteristics, since they have the same genetic makeup.
   d. Motor ability, age, and experience might all be important variables that would be controlled by using the identical twins who would likely have the same experiences from similar environments as well as the identical genes.

## Post Test

1. The original pair of populations is converted to a single population.
2. The standard error is smaller when the two samples are dependent.
3. $n - 1$
4. Subjects may be lost. It is costly and time-consuming.
5. It reduces the size of the estimated standard error.
6. Matching is appropriate only when an uncontrolled variable has been identified that aids in the interpretation of the preliminary findings.

7. Repeated measures is a special case where the same subjects are used in both samples.
8. The assumption is that the population of difference scores is normally distributed.
9. The result is relatively unaffected if sample size is sufficiently large.
10. The assumptions are that the population distributions for $X$ and $Y$ are normally distributed and the relationship between $X$ and $Y$ is linear.

# Chapter 21

## Text Review

1. *p*-values
2. rejected
3. retained
4. *p*-values
5. borderline
6. type II
7. null
8. excessively large
9. point biserial
10. independent

## Problems and Exercises

1. a. p < .01     b. yes for .01, no for .001
2. a,c,d
3. a. .05
   b. Yes, it would say there is **NOT** a statistical difference because p is not less than .001.
4. $r^2 = .0187$
   a. small effect
   b. Could lack practical importance unless there are special circumstances.

## Post Test

| 1. false | 2. true | 3. true | 4. true | 5. false |
|----------|---------|---------|---------|----------|
| 6. true | 7. false | 8. false | 9. false | 10. true |

# Chapter 22

## Text Review

1. analysis of variance
2. one-way
3. chance
4. false
5. treatment effect
6. random error
7. error term
8. variability
9. degrees of freedom
10. mean square
11. differently
12. similarly
13. random error
14. treatment effect
15. normally distributed
16. 10
17. effect size
18. multiple comparisons
19. type I
20. level of significance
21. nondirectional

## Problems and Exercises

1. Which of the three methods tested is the most effective in improving reading?
   Statistical hypotheses:
   $H_0$: $\mu_{tutoring} = \mu_{home\ help} = \mu_{reading\ aloud}$
   $H_1$: $H_0$ is false.
   Decision rule: Reject $H_0$ at the .05 level of significance if $F$ equals or is more positive than 3.38, given $df_{between} = 2$ and $df_{within} = 25$.
   $F = 15.107$
   Decision: Reject $H_0$.
   Interpretation: There is evidence that one or more of the reading methods improves reading more than the others.

| Source | SS | Df | MS | F |
|--------|--------|----|--------|--------|
| Between | 100.19 | 2 | 50.060 | 15.107 |
| Within | 82.844 | 25 | 3.314 | |
| Total | 182.964 | 27 | | |

Scheffe's test may be used.
$\mu_1 - \mu_2$ = significant difference
$\mu_1 - \mu_3$ = significant difference
$\mu_2 - \mu_3$ = not a significant difference

2. Which of the four methods tested is the most effective in reducing blood pressure?

   Statistical hypotheses:

   $H_0$: $\mu_{control} = \mu_{medication} = \mu_{exercise} = \mu_{meditation}$

   $H_1$: $H_0$ is false.

   Decision rule:

   Reject $H_0$ at the .05 level of significance if $F$ equals or is more positive than 2.88, given $df_{between}$ = 3 and $df_{within}$ = 34.

   $F = 57.42$

   Decision: Reject $H_0$.

   Interpretation: There is evidence that one or more of the methods is better at reducing blood pressure.

   | Source | SS | Df | MS | F |
   |--------|------|----|--------|-------|
   | Between | 604.92 | 3 | 201.64 | 57.42 |
   | Within | 119.40 | 34 | 3.51 | |
   | Total | 724.32 | 37 | | |

   Scheffe's test may be used.
   $\mu_1$ vs $\mu_2$ = significant difference
   $\mu_1$ vs $\mu_3$ = significant difference
   $\mu_1$ vs $\mu_4$ = significant difference
   $\mu_2$ vs $\mu_3$ = significant difference
   $\mu_2$ vs $\mu_4$ = significant difference
   $\mu_3$ vs $\mu_4$ = not a significant difference

3. The group receiving no treatment allows the researcher to establish what changes in blood pressure might occur just with the passing of time. It serves as a measure of control.

## Post Test

1. The null hypothesis is retained.
2. Variability between will exceed variability within.
3. Treatment effect exists.
4. Through use of multiple comparison tests such as Scheffe's test.
5. Only when the null hypothesis is rejected.
6. Because all values are squared and thus positive.
7. Underlying populations are normally distributed and have equal variances.
8. No problem would exist as long as sample sizes are sufficiently large.
9. If sample sizes are equal, only one critical value must be calculated, and all pairs may be compared using that value.
10. The researcher uses the squared curvilinear correlation when the null hypothesis has been rejected and applies Cohen's rule of thumb in order to estimate the size of the effect.

# Chapter 23

## Text Review

1. gender
2. chance
3. main effect
4. main effect
5. grand mean
6. variability
7. treatment effect
8. random error
9. interaction
10. inconsistent
11. underlying
12. equal
13. sample sizes
14. mean squares
15. degrees of freedom
16. sum of squares
17. rejection
18. row means

## Problems and Exercises

1.

| Source | SS | Df | MS | F |
|---|---|---|---|---|
| Column | 93.8 | 2 | 46.9 | 6.34 |
| Row | 22.5 | 1 | 22.5 | 3.04 |
| Interaction | 388.1 | 2 | 194.1 | 26.23 |
| Within | 178.4 | 24 | 7.4 | |
| Total | 682.8 | 29 | | |

2.

| Source | SS | Df | MS | F |
|---|---|---|---|---|
| Column | .2 | 1 | .2 | .04 |
| Row | 0 | 1 | .00 | .00 |
| Interaction | 23.9 | 1 | 23.9 | 4.35 |
| Within | 109.7 | 20 | 5.5 | |
| Total | 133.8 | 23 | | |

## Post Test

1. Slanted lines indicate a possible main effect; parallel lines indicate a possible interaction.
2. The numerator represents variability between groups, columns, rows, and variability due to interaction. The denominator represents the variability within groups or random error.
3. A calculated value of $F$ is compared to a critical value of $F$, and if the calculated value exceeds the critical value, the null hypothesis is rejected.
4. Interaction.
5. The assumptions for the $F$ test in two-way ANOVA are that underlying populations are normally distributed and have equal variances.
6. There is no concern for violations of these assumptions if sample size is larger than 10.

# Chapter 24

## Text Review

1. qualitative
2. proportions
3. expected frequency
4. rejected
5. negative
6. categories
7. positive
8. two-way
9. independent
10. 5
11. Cramer's

## Problems and Exercises

1. $X^2 = 3.31$     $df = 2, p > .10$     retain $H_0$
2. $X^2 = 1.12$     $df = 3, p > .10$     retain $H_0$
3. $X^2 = 4.72$     $df = 1, p < .05$     reject $H_0$
   There is evidence that religious preference is related to attitude toward abortion $[X^2 (1, n = 150) = 4.72, p < .05]$.
4. $X^2 = 4.58$,    $df = 3, p > .10$, retain $H_0$
   There is no evidence that type of student is related to preference for instructional method $[X^2 (3, n = 100) = 4.58, p > .10]$.

## Post Test

1. One-way test
2. Two-way test
3. Because all discrepancies are squared, so there can never be a negative value.
4. The conditions for using the chi-square test are (1) all observations must be independent, (2) expected frequencies must be sufficiently large, and (3) sample size must be neither too small nor too large.
5. The expected frequency is the hypothesized frequency for a category that the researcher expects to obtain. The observed frequency is the actual observed frequency for each category.

6. The researcher uses the squared Cramer's phi coefficient when the null hypothesis has been rejected and applies Cohen's rule of thumb in order to estimate the strength of the relationship.

# Chapter 25

## Text Review

| | |
|---|---|
| 1. ranked | 2. parameter |
| 3. distribution-free | 4. equal |
| 5. ranked | 6. quantitative |
| 7. type II error | 8. normality |
| 9. type I error | 10. distributions |
| 11. means | 12. rejected |
| 13. less | 14. variabilities |
| 15. shapes | 16. uncontrolled |
| 17. normality | 18. entire populations |
| 19. nondirectional | 20. less |
| 21. normality | 22. variances |
| 23. nondirectional | |

## Problems and Exercises

1. Using a one-tailed test, $U = 3$, reject $H_o$, $p < .01$
   There is evidence that parental training in behavior modification influences first graders' compliance with teacher requests.
2. Using a one-tailed test, $T = 0$, reject $H_o$, $p < .01$
   The evidence suggests that therapy and workshops helped reduce anxiety.
3. $H = 21.95$, $df = 4$, reject $H_o$, $p < .05$
   The evidence suggests that movies with different ratings contain different numbers of expletives.
4. $H = 15.697$, $df = 2$, reject $H_o$, $p < .05$
   The evidence suggests that the reading methods differ in improving the reading of third graders.

## Post Test

1. Mann-Whitney $U$ test
2. Wilcoxon $T$ test
3. These tests must be used when the data are ranked or the assumptions of normality and equal variances in the populations are violated.

4. In the decision rule for each of these tests, the null hypothesis is rejected if the observed value is less than or equal to the critical value.
5. Nonparametric tests are those such as $U$, $T$, and $H$, which evaluate entire population distributions rather than specific population characteristics.
6. Distribution-free tests are those, such as $U$, $T$, and $H$, which make no assumptions about the form of the population distribution.
7. Kruskal-Wallis $H$ test

# Chapter 26

## Text Review

1. descriptive
2. inferential
3. confidence interval
4. quantitative
5. qualitative
6. *t*
7. ANOVA
8. two-way
9. ranked

## Problems and Exercise

1. Correlation—Pearson *r*
2. *t* test for independent samples
3. *t* test for dependent samples
4. two-way chi-square
5. one-way *F*
6. one-way *F*
7. Mann-Whitney *U* test
8. *t* test for independent samples
9. Correlation—Pearson *r*
10. one-way *F*

Printed in the United States
34417LVS00004B/83-164

9 780470 004067